BONE

CAGE

BONE CAGE

BY CATHERINE BANKS

Playwrights Canada Press
Toronto • Canada

PLAYWRIGHTS CANADA PRESS
The Canadian Drama Publisher
215 Spadina Ave., Suite 230, Toronto, Ontario, Canada, M5T 2C7
phone 416.703.0013   fax 416.408.3402
orders@playwrightscanada.com • www.playwrightscanada.com

The publisher acknowledges the support of the Canadian taxpayers through the Government of Canada Book Publishing Industry Development Program, the Canada Council for the Arts, the Ontario Arts Council, and the Ontario Media Development Corporation.

Front cover painting "Flooded Stand of Pine" by Karen Klee-Atlin. Acrylic on wood, 45 x 45 x 9 cm, 2007.
Cover Design and Production Editor: JLArt

LIBRARY AND ARCHIVES CANADA CATALOGUING IN PUBLICATION

Banks, Catherine
Bone cage / Catherine Banks.

A play.

ISBN 978-0-88754-787-4
I. Title.

PS8553.A5635B65 2008   C812'.54   C2008-903421-X

First edition: June 2008.
Second Printing: April 2009.
Printed and bound by Canadian Printco Ltd. at Scarborough, Canada.

The poem "Bird Cage", F.R. Scott's translation of "Cage d'Oiseau"
by Saint-Denys Garneau is used with the permission of
William Toye, Literary Executor to the Estate of F. R. Scott.

To my children, Rilla and Simon, with love.

There are men of the valley
Who are that valley.
                    —Wallace Stevens

Acknowledgements

To Tessa Mendel, who both dramaturged and directed the first production of *Bone Cage*. Thank you for your tough, insightful questions. Your unwavering belief in my work these past fifteen years has been a lifeline.

This play was written with the support of the Canada Council for the Arts. A first draft of *Bone Cage* was commissioned by Mulgrave Road Theatre through a Nova Scotia Arts Commissioning grant.

The playwright gratefully acknowledges the support of Playwrights Atlantic Resource Centre, the National Arts Centre's On the Verge 2005, Exodus Theatre, ScriptLab (Toronto), Playwrights Workshop Montreal, Theatre B.C. National Play Competition 2002, Forerunner Playwrights Co-op, Ship's Company Theatre, and Nova Scotia Tourism, Culture and Heritage.

Special thanks to: Andrea Dymond, Natasha MacLellan, Pamela Halstead, Tessa Mendel, Philip Adams, Jenny Munday, Paula Danckert, Janis Spence, Leah Hamilton, Laura McLauchlan, Karen Klee Atlin, Lenora Steele, Chris Heide, John Dunsworth, Christine Birnie, Angela Rebeiro, Annie Gibson, Jodi Armstrong, Don Hannah, Peter Rogers, Garnet C. Banks, Tom Banks, Dan and Diana Banks, Claudia Mitchell and my parents Garnet and Kathleen Banks.

Bone Cage was first produced by Forerunner Playwrights Co-op, in partnership with Ship's Company Theatre, at the Neptune Studio, Halifax, Nova Scotia, October 10–14, 2007 with the following company:

JAMIE	Michael McPhee
CHICKY	Kate Lavender*
KRISTA	Caitlin Stewart
KEVIN	John-Riley O'Handley
ROBBY	Matthew Lumley
CLARENCE	Hugo Dann*
LISSA	Sarah English

Director: Tessa Mendel
Stage Manager: Kay Robertson*
Set, Poster and Props Design: Corey Mullins
Lighting Design: Leigh Ann Vardy with associate Tom Barkley
Original Score and Sound Design: Terry Pulliam
Costumes Design: Andrea Ritchie

*appeared with permission of Canadian Actors' Equity Association

• • •

Bone Cage was presented as a staged reading at the National Arts Centre, Ottawa, on June 16, 2005, as part of On the Verge 2005 with the following company:

JAMIE	Benjamin Meuser
CHICKY	Laura Teasdale
KRISTA	Catriona Leger
KEVIN	Mark Muntean
ROBBY	Daniel Giverin
CLARENCE	Robert Welch
LISSA	Rachel Scott-Mignon

Director: Tessa Mendel
Stage Manager: Lynn Cox
Artistic Coordinator: Lise Ann Johnson

Characters

JAMIE, twenty-two, works a tree processor
CHICKY, twenty-five, Jamie's half sister, works on the sod fields
KRISTA, seventeen, Jamie's girlfriend, in high school
KEVIN, eighteen, Krista's brother, works chainsaw
CLARENCE, fifty-two, Jamie's father, on disability
ROBBY, thirty, considered slow, works for Chicky's married lover
LISSA, fourteen, Robby's sister, slow

Note about the Text

When an italized word appears in brackets it is not meant to be spoken, but rather inform the actor of the character's feeling at that moment. When one appears at the end of a line following an ellipsis "…" it is the next word the actor would have spoken.

BONE CAGE

ACT I

Scene 1

Lights up to half. JAMIE sits on the rail of a steel bridge painted industrial green.

JAMIE is stroking the body of a dead blue jay. It is early morning and he has just come off the night shift in the tree processor.

There is the sound of a huge pulp truck travelling on a village road. The sound of it approaching, then the swamped noise of it passing too fast, and too close. The engine accelerates as it struggles up a steep hill and then fades as it leaves the village.

JAMIE
Oh yeah.

Everything in its path it eats.
Yellow birch   spruce   fir
White maple
It picks its teeth with the alders.
Bitter taste don't matter.
Eats squirrels, porkies.
Mainly birds, lots still in the nests.

He holds up the jay looking at it carefully.

Not so safe after all.

To the tree processor
I'm the first beer of the day.
What's needed to get it started.

At the end of every shift
It pisses me out on the ground.

I saw an eastern ghost once.
A cougar, watching me in the woods.
Biologists say cougars don't exist around here.

That's funny because I saw one
And he saw me too.

I said,
"You do exist same as me."
And he said back, "There you have it, Jamie-boy."
When I got a kid someday
Just born and everything
I'm going to go raid that fox den
That I know where it's at
And go get a cub.
Foxes are always black when they're cubs.
And I'm going to raise the baby and that fox up together.
Fox curl up in the crib at night
Baby play out in the woods all day
'Til their hair grows orange.
And their second teeth?
Razor sharp.

> *JAMIE drops the dead bird off the bridge into the river.*

Scene 2

> *Lights up.*

> *CHICKY sits next to the river.*

CHICKY
I don't know how my head gets tired mowing sod fields but it does.
It hurts all day like when I was waiting for Trav's next breath, and
then the next one.
There's this elm tree on the edge of the river
I mow past fifty times a day.
It's dead, been dead for a few years like all the elms.
This tree looks exactly like a scarred, burnt-out woman.
An old woman who had twenty kids and they all died of cancer of
the brain while she was at the store.
The branches are broken off 'n what's left looks like arms thrust over
her head, panicked.
Where her breasts were are these two gaping holes and she's got
a bigger hole that looks like a vagina opening up, only its below her
ribs like where Christ was wounded.

She's got a face too.
The peckers have been at her but she got these two eyes and the bark
below them is buckled, like a mouth getting ready for a good bellow.
"I told you to stay away from the goddamn river."

There's a lot of power in her anyway
and she's not too happy with me.
Rolling up the sod, taking up a layer of soil every time.
I tell her it's a job so I can stay.
She tells me it's my soul.

My soul, I tell her, isn't worth anything.
She knows that because I've told her everything in the last three
years as I've mowed past her.
I've showed her all my *(pause)* warts, let's just say.
But still she waves those old arms at me
tells me I'm peeling away my only hope of *redemption*
thin layer by thin layer.

> *The lights expand to show KRISTA, standing behind CHICKY,*
> *fumbling with a tightly rolled square of paper. JAMIE and KEVIN*
> *are sitting up on the bridge. The distance is suggested by the fact*
> *KRISTA and CHICKY must shout up to the boys to be heard.*
>
> *This is their summer hangout. They know this place like they know*
> *their own bodies. It is Saturday just before noon.*

KRISTA
  (reading) "Love…
  Is patient and kind: love is not
  Jealous, or conceited, or proud,
  Or provoked; love does not keep
  A record of wrongs; love is not
  Happy with evil, but is pleased
  With the truth…"

CHICKY
  Krista what is that?

KRISTA
  It's our scroll.

  (reading) "Love never gives
  Up: its faith, hope and patience never fail.
  Thank you for sharing with us every

Precious moment of this day.
Jamie and Krista."

It'll be rolled up by the plate and have a fuchsia ribbon tied onto it.

CHICKY
Do we always have to talk about the wedding?

KRISTA
Excuse me for wanting a perfect wedding day.
(pause) My guts are tender. I must be ovulating.

CHICKY
Krista if you aren't having your period or PMS then you're
ovulating, or you got break-through bleeding.

KRISTA
Doctor can't find no reason for it.
The doctor told me to go off the pill soon as I can.

CHICKY
You said you didn't want kids 'til you build.

KRISTA
When we're married we can use something else.

CHICKY
What difference will *being married* make?

KRISTA
It will is all.

CHICKY
Yeah right. You hear anything about Carol from anybody?

KRISTA
No. Like what?

CHICKY
Nothing. Nothing I said.

KRISTA
You got some dances in last night.

CHICKY
Two fast ones.

KRISTA
Reg's not going to slow dance you with Carol standing right there.

CHICKY
Reg slow dances Carol with me standing right there.

KRISTA
Even if they don't have sex anymore, she is his wife.

CHICKY laughs.

What?

CHICKY
You are going to be just like all the rest you know.
Soon as you're a wife I'll be the enemy.

KRISTA
I told ya I won't be. You won't be.

CHICKY
Okay. You going for a swim?

KRISTA
No, I think I'm ovulating.

CHICKY
(Jesus.)

KEVIN sits to the left of JAMIE. He has his arm hooked around the side rail of the bridge. He is unable to unhook his arm for any reason, as he is afraid of heights. JAMIE is the ultimate cool to KEVIN'S excitement.

KEVIN
God that was fucking hilarious last night.
(What?)
Stealing Dolores's flower box and dragging it to the diner.
Je*sus* were the sparks flying.
Practically tore the fucking bumper off the car remember?
(No?)
Duh-your-ass, Dolores? *(Remember?)* Duh your assssss.
Fuck.
Funniest idea you ever had. *(FUCK.)*

Hey Chicky… skinny dip… skinny dip skinny dip.

JAMIE
Is that all you think about – getting girls to take their clothes off?

KEVIN

Yeah.

Wouldn't mind seeing Chicky skinny dip.

JAMIE

She's too old for you, Kev. I saw Lissa at the store, she's getting some nice apples on her.

KEVIN

She's like fourteen.

JAMIE

Get them young, while they're fresh.

KEVIN

Chicky and me got some excellent dances in last night. Slow ones. She asked me.

JAMIE

You're frigging eighteen, she's twenty-five.

KEVIN

That means we are both at our sexual peak.

JAMIE

Shit. Anyway, old Reggie's got his finger in her pie.
Stole her cherry when she was fifteen.

KEVIN

She's your sister, for Chrissake.

JAMIE

She's my half sister. What's she to you? *(pause)*
Hey chicky chicky chicky, Kev's got a hard-on for you.

KEVIN

Shut up.

JAMIE

She can't hear me. Hey Chicky. *Chicky.*

CHICKY

What?

JAMIE

Kevin wants a date, don't you, Kev?
Well, he's too fucking shy to ask but he does.

CHICKY
Fuzzy, lay off him.

> *JAMIE makes kissing noises back at her.*

How's your head, anyway?

> *JAMIE toasts her by opening a new beer.*

JAMIE
My head is just fine.

CHICKY
Jesus. Do you see what you're marrying?

KRISTA
He looks some handsome in his tux, wait 'til you see him.

> *ROBBY enters wheeling a bike. Stands looking over the side of the bridge.*

CHICKY
Hey, Robby.

ROBBY
Hi, Chic-ky

KEVIN
(*mimics*) Hi, Chic-ky.

JAMIE
If it isn't a member of the social gimp family.

CHICKY
Shut up.

JAMIE
What? Being a social gimp is a good thing isn't it, Kev?

CHICKY
You two shut up.
You haying for Reg next week, Robby?

ROBBY
Driving the John Deere tractor.

JAMIE
Didn't Reg tell you, RobBob, he's using oxen this year!

ROBBY
No he ain't.

CHICKY
Don't be so goddamn mean.

JAMIE
RobBob knows I'm jokin' with him, don't ya, RobBob?

ROBBY
Someone took Mom's flower box last night – dragged it way down to the diner.

JAMIE
Oh my God, is that right?

ROBBY
Left it at the diner.

JAMIE
Who did that?

ROBBY
I know.

JAMIE
Oh you *think* you know, do you?

KEVIN
Tell us.

ROBBY
I know who did. I'm not telling.

JAMIE
Good thing.

ROBBY
I know who did it.
Woke Mom up.
Woke Lissa up.
Yelled at us.
Break the porch light.
Take Mom's flower box. I know it.

JAMIE
But you're not telling right?

ROBBY
> Gonna do something if they don't stop.

JAMIE
> I bet they're scared, whoever they are.

ROBBY
> Make them sorry. Make them be sorry.

> *ROBBY turns and rides off.*

JAMIE
> Well, I'm shaking, what about you, Kev?

CHICKY
> You guys!

JAMIE
> Did he say it was us?

CHICKY
> If it wasn't the two of you, who was it?

JAMIE
> How the hell should I know?

CHICKY
> Leave them alone. They don't hurt anybody.

JAMIE
> Jesus, how many times have I got to say it wasn't us!

CHICKY
> Kev, you take it back today.

JAMIE
> Yes, Kev, you do that.

KEVIN
> I think it might be pretty hard on the bumper, Jamie.

JAMIE
> Hell, I'll take the tractor and charge Robbie's old man twenty bucks.

CHICKY
> Fuzzy!

JAMIE

I'm funnin' ya. I'll build them a goddamn new flower box, how's that?

CHICKY

You should!

KRISTA

Maybe it wasn't Jamie and Kev.

CHICKY

Krista, look at them.

KRISTA

I'm just saying, Robbie could be confused.

CHICKY

He isn't retarded and *he* wouldn't hurt a fly. Lissa is sweet and good. Dolores's house is the cleanest in the village. They run a farm. They're good workers.

KRISTA

Well, they're not too bright.

CHICKY

How in the hell would anyone in this place know? The most intelligent person in the world could live next to them and they wouldn't know it. A saint could move into the village and no one would give a shit. Mother Theresa could rise from the dead, go to a dance at the firehall to bless the goddamn works of them, and I bet all Jamie would do is crack jokes about her tits.

JAMIE starts walking along the bridge rail.

KRISTA

Why are you so down on him? To me, too.
I'm marrying him in six days you know.

CHICKY

It's not too late to change your mind.

KRISTA notices JAMIE.

KRISTA

Sit down, Jamie.

CHICKY

You know he's going to do it if you watch him.

KRISTA

Well I told him when we're married he ain't jumping off the high no more.

CHICKY

When you two are married it will be you up there doing the death dance.

Hey, Kev!

Kevin. Hey!

JAMIE

Hey, Kev, she wants you, man.

CHICKY

Throw me a smoke.

> *JAMIE sits down. KEVIN takes out a smoke without letting go of the bridge.*
>
> *There is the sound of a car engine wide open squealing through the village.*

JAMIE

F'ing Merv asshole.

A-HOLE!

KEVIN

They asked me up to their camp tonight.

JAMIE

Merv did?

KEVIN

Not just Merv, there's a bunch of them.

JAMIE

That's one place you don't want to go.

KEVIN

Just a bunch playing cards.

JAMIE

They're looking for someone to get ugly at.

CHICKY

Kev, my smoke.

KEVIN
>It's coming.

>>*He throws one but CHICKY steps on it by mistake.*

>Shit.
>They just drink and play cards.

>>*He throws down the package with the lighter tucked inside.*

JAMIE
>Don't go.

KEVIN
>You go.

JAMIE
>Yeah but I'm me and you're you.
>You go up there and you'll come home one sorry ass.

KEVIN
>I'm not going to fight nobody.

JAMIE
>You go up there and I'll beat the crap out of you myself.

KEVIN
>Fuck you. I can go anywhere I want. I can take care of myself.

JAMIE
>So you think.

KEVIN
>Yeah well, I know something about you, don't I?

JAMIE
>What?

KEVIN
>I ain't telling.

>>*JAMIE shifts his weight so he is within striking distance of KEVIN, while pretending to hand him an empty beer bottle.*

JAMIE
>Is it about my stag?

KEVIN
>Maybe. Maybe not. I ain't telling you.

JAMIE
I'm going to be your sweet brother-in-law, you better tell me.

KEVIN
F you!

> *JAMIE grabs KEVIN and pulls him into a headlock. He begins to tug on KEVIN's arm to get him away from his hold on the bridge.*

I ain't telling you.

> *JAMIE succeeds in pulling him from the side.*

JAMIE
Hope you can swim.

> *KEVIN is very afraid.*

KEVIN
Let go of me, man.

JAMIE
Think you know where that little hole is, that you've got to hit when you jump from here, or else your spine goes...

> *JAMIE snaps his fingers in quick succession as KEVIN struggles.*

Just like that!

KEVIN
Let go let go let go of me.

KRISTA
Kev, you come down here.

CHICKY
Krista! Christ, Jamie's throwing Kevin off the bridge, not the other way 'round.

Fuzzy! *Jamie.* Let him alone *right now*!

JAMIE
She wants me to let go of you, Kev, should I?

KEVIN
I'm going to fall, Jamie... I'm gonna fall!

JAMIE
Better tell me.

KEVIN
It ain't about your stag, okay?

JAMIE
What then?
What, Kev, I'll drop you.

KEVIN
I'll tell ya, I'll *tell* ya. I'm telling you, man. Just don't get mad at me when you hear it.

JAMIE
You tell me, I'll decide who to get mad at.

KEVIN I heard Earl saying at the dance that he's putting you on chainsaw for the summer.

JAMIE
No he ain't. You don't make shit on chainsaw.

KEVIN
Starting the Monday after your wedding, he said.

JAMIE fakes it one last time like he's going to drop KEVIN, then slowly lets go of him.

JAMIE
That's funny, I'm giving my week's notice this Monday.

KEVIN scrambles out of reach.

CHICKY
Kevin, get your ass down here.

JAMIE
She wants your ass, Kev.

KEVIN
You can't quit, Krista will kill you.

JAMIE
She don't need to know.

KEVIN
She's marrying you on Saturday.

JAMIE
A lot can happen in a week. In a week I might be the head of IBM.

KEVIN
He said the next time you quit, he wouldn't take you back.

JAMIE
I don't do dumb-ass work.

KEVIN
I'd rather work chainsaw.
Freaked me out too bad, that one time in the processor.
Everything tore up so bad, I couldn't find my way out.
Four hours lost in the woods.

JAMIE
I leave a tree standing where I go in.

KEVIN
Anyway, Earl won't take you back.

JAMIE
Earl don't have shit left to log.

> *JAMIE hands KEVIN a newspaper clipping.*

KEVIN
(reading) "Heli-logging. Training for men and women in an exciting high-paying career in B.C.'s Forestry Industry. Comprehensive three-month heli-pilot training program."

Like Krista's going to leave the Valley and move out there.

JAMIE
Krista. *Krista!*

KRISTA
Get down here, Jamie, we've got to get to town.

JAMIE
A wife has to go where her husband goes, right?

KRISTA
Is he going to town?

JAMIE
A wife *has to go* where her husband goes, right?

KRISTA
Jaaaaaaaaaaamie, come on!

JAMIE

You better answer yes, or this wedding is off.

KRISTA

Yes. Okay, yes. Now can we go to town?

CHICKY

Fuzzy, did you make that call?

JAMIE

You shut your trap about any call, sis. I mean it, too.

CHICKY

Krista, aren't you curious about this call I'm not supposed to talk about?

KRISTA

Is it about my wedding present from Jamie?

CHICKY

Oh—*(Christ)*. Has Jamie talked about quitting?

KRISTA

He'd better not. I got to pay for the hall and the supper with his next cheque. *(urgent)* Jamie.

> *CHICKY slips on her shoes and prepares to leave.*

JAMIE

Where you going, Chicky?

CHICKY

Home to feed *your* father.

JAMIE

Let the whore come and cook his dinner.

CHICKY

That's our mother you're talking about.

JAMIE

(lightly) Your mother is a whore. My mother is a fucking whore.

CHICKY

Do you ever listen to what comes out of his mouth?

KRISTA

Well, your mom has lived with a lot of men.

uvic bookstore

3800 FINNERTY RD. VICTORIA BC V8W 3H6

THANK YOU FOR SHOPPING WITH US

CHICKY
(Jesus).

KRISTA
She left you kids when Travis was a toddler, what kind of mother does that?

CHICKY
Okay, I'm going now.

KEVIN
You leaving, Chicky?

CHICKY
I should have been leaving when I got here. I got four hours mowing yet, Reg's stripping sod on Friday.

JAMIE
Hey! I ain't ready to go.

CHICKY
I'm walking.

KEVIN
I'll walk with you.

JAMIE
Kevin wants a blow job.

KEVIN
Shut up.

JAMIE
I said "new job," Kevin wants a new job, *a nude job.*
(laughs) Hey, sis. Save me some dinner.

CHICKY
Why should I?

JAMIE
'Cause I'm your little brother, and you've got to take care of me.

CHICKY
Starting Saturday, I don't, do I?

KRISTA
Call me.

CHICKY and KEVIN leave.

You coming down?
Jamie?
We got stuff to do in town today.

JAMIE

Like what?

KRISTA

Like I already said.

>   *JAMIE comes down.*

You've got to pick up the washing machine, too.

JAMIE

Don't know why you're buying their shit.

KRISTA

Dolores is getting her mother's.

JAMIE

Dolores is getting her mother's.

KRISTA

You're in a pissy mood.

JAMIE

I'm ovulating.

KRISTA

A new one would cost us seven hundred dollars.

JAMIE

Wash at your mother's.

KRISTA

I'm not doing that, I told you.

JAMIE

I got no place to store a washer.

KRISTA

Take it to the trailer!

JAMIE

Can't.

KRISTA

You didn't get the key from Danny yet?

JAMIE

Nope.

KRISTA

He was supposed to move out two weeks ago. He knows we're getting married this week. You told him he had to move out. Why ain't he moved out?

JAMIE

I'll take it home for now.

KRISTA

Does Danny think he is going to live with us?
I'm calling him and telling him he's got to be out tomorrow.

JAMIE

I told him he could have the trailer until October.

KRISTA

Yeah, right.

JAMIE

That's twenty-five hundred in cash.

KRISTA

No way. Jamie, where are we supposed to live? Not with your father.

JAMIE

He knows to leave us alone.

KRISTA

He hates my guts. He don't speak to me.

JAMIE

We need the money, okay? Every time I turn around you need money for invitations, to rent the hall, to rent white fucking tuxedos to go with the fucking bought bridesmaid off-the-shoulder cocktail-length fucking dress. Then there's the turkey sit-down meal and four hundred and fifty for the fucking DJ?

KRISTA

I don't want to live with Clarence.

JAMIE

Krista, the trailer is worth more to us rented. We rent to Danny for a few months, we've got enough to get somewhere.

KRISTA
I told you I don't want a honeymoon. It don't matter to me.

JAMIE
I told Danny he has it.
Fuck. You love me or you don't.

KRISTA
I'm marrying you aren't I?

KRISTA kisses him playfully until he responds a little.

Weddings cost money.

JAMIE
We'll have enough by Christmas.

KRISTA
Christmas? Jamie!

JAMIE
I promise. I do I do I do.

He starts to crow like a rooster. He does a sort of endearing rooster dance. KRISTA laughs. He kisses her hungrily.

KRISTA
No. Jamie, we have to go to town.

JAMIE
I can't wait.

KRISTA
Not here.

JAMIE
Why not?

KRISTA
Robby might come back, or anybody.

JAMIE
So, never stopped us before.

KRISTA
Wellllll… I've been thinking.
The wedding is Saturday.
Maybe we shouldn't, you know, make love until our wedding night.

JAMIE

Funny.

KRISTA

To make it more special.

JAMIE

Krista hon-ey!

KRISTA

Please.

JAMIE

Okay, starting Friday night.

KRISTA

I'm spotting.

JAMIE

Christ.

KRISTA

He said we have to go off the pill after we're married.

JAMIE

This wedding is really starting to suck the big one.

KRISTA

Don't say that.

JAMIE

It's not like not doing it is gonna turn you into a virgin.

KRISTA

Okay, let's do it, so we can get to town.

JAMIE

What about the... *(spotting)*

KRISTA

It don't hurt or nothing, just spotting a bit.

JAMIE

Baby, I wouldn't last seven days! You make me wait that long, and the minute you say I do, I'll be on you. The minister will be saying, "I said kiss the bride, not screw her."

KRISTA

I hate it when you call it that.

JAMIE

Sorrrry. I said to kiss her not make love to her. Make love to her. Make lovvveee to her.

JAMIE kisses her grandly until she is laughing.

Oh, baby, you know what I like.

KRISTA

Soon as we're married I'm divorcing you.

JAMIE pulls her down on the sand.

KRISTA takes the hunting knife off his belt and holds it to her mouth. Her tongue touches the tip.

JAMIE

Why do you like that? Doing it with the knife?

She lays the knife carefully beside them. She begins to kiss him.

KRISTA

It makes it more fun.
It makes it fun-er.

They kiss.

Lights down.

Scene 3

CLARENCE sits in his chair with his ear to the phone.

CLARENCE

Betty? You didn't let me finish. I'm saying they got places now, not like when Trav died, there are places now. I'm just saying don't cremate him, because then you got no cells, no DNA.

CHICKY comes in.

(pause) Yeah, Ronnie, I was explaining it to Betty. I'm not trying to kill her with nonsense. I'm trying to be a good neighbour, to give her scientific information…. It's been on "Oprah," it's been on "Larry King Live," Je*sus* I'm giving ya hope…

The phone has obviously been disconnected.

CHICKY
You've got to stop calling Betty.

CLARENCE
I been wondering if there was going to be any dinner around here.

CHICKY
You heard me.

CLARENCE
They should have flown him straight to Florida.

CHICKY
For Chrissakes Clarence. The woman's lost a child. She's beside herself.
You should know that.

CLARENCE
I do know. I do know.
I'm telling her they got *equipment* down there.

CHICKY
He's dead. He died at the scene.

CLARENCE
They put them in liquid oxygen. Twenty-five years from now they'll have a cure for it.

CHICKY
There is no cure for a ten-year-old, without a helmet, flying off the back of a dirt bike onto the highway. Don't call Betty again.

> *CLARENCE sulks. But he has news that he can't hold back on.*

CLARENCE
I got something in the mail today.
I got something to show you, Chicky.

CHICKY
I thought you wanted your dinner.

CLARENCE
Look, I got it right here.
Here.

> *CLARENCE opens a large brown envelope and takes out a pencil drawing of a young man of about nineteen.*

CHICKY
Who's that supposed to be?

CLARENCE
It's an artist rendition.
Read the back.

CHICKY
(reading) "Extend Your Memory is proud to present you with this portrait of your son…"

CLARENCE
Travis, *yes!*
Jesus, didn't you recognize our little Trav?

CHICKY stares at the drawing.

It's what he'd look like today. I sent that school picture of Trav before he got sick to this artist in the States, and that fellow took it and drew him nine years older.

CHICKY gives the drawing back to CLARENCE.

He looks good don't he?

CHICKY
How much?

CLARENCE
Don't matter.

CHICKY
We still owe on the headstone. What did Jamie say?

CLARENCE
I'm telling Jamie I'm paying for it out of my disability.

CHICKY
Yeah, you pay for that, then we pay for your smokes.

CLARENCE
Where you been half the day anyway?

CHICKY
At the river with Jamie.

CLARENCE
Ain't he working?

JAMIE comes in. CLARENCE quickly tucks the picture out of sight.

CHICKY
Apparently no.
Thought you were taking Krista to town?

JAMIE
I am. I had to check on Sky. He's off his food.

CLARENCE
A bird can't survive after hittin' a power line. Not even a big bird like him.

JAMIE
Vet said he could. He had been eating good.
The burn is healing up.

CLARENCE
Eagles that can't fly lose their will to live.

JAMIE
Like a man that can't work, right, Clarence?

CHICKY
Speaking of work, are you working nights this week?

JAMIE
Depends. Might be laid off.

CHICKY
I haven't heard that Earl is laying off men.

JAMIE
I don't work chainsaw.

CHICKY
(hopeful) You're quitting?

CLARENCE
He's being laid off, didn't you hear him? People don't listen. Oprah had a man on there who said mothers talk to their kids five minutes a day. That's a God-awful thing. Don't know their kids from their own assholes.

JAMIE
From a man who hasn't used his asshole in ten years.

CHICKY
Don't start on him.

JAMIE
Five minutes is about four minutes and thirty seconds longer than we ever talked, Dad.

CLARENCE
Used to talk before you know who came along.

JAMIE
Get real.

CLARENCE
You used to watch the games with me.

JAMIE
That ain't talking, Dad. Okay, Chicky, time us.

CLARENCE
I got nothing to say.

JAMIE
Ask me about my job.

CLARENCE
You just said.

JAMIE
Ask me how my job makes me feel. Does it make me feel important or *(leans hard here)* fulfilled, or does it make me feel like a pile of steaming yellow s-h-i-t.

CLARENCE
I ain't talking to you when you're in a mood.

CLARENCE turns up the TV volume.

JAMIE winds up like he is going to kick the screen in, then stops and taps the off button with his boot toe.

JAMIE
Time please.

CHICKY
Fuzzy. Fifteen seconds, okay?

JAMIE
Oprah, be proud of us.

JAMIE turns the TV on. He heads out the door.

CLARENCE
You going to town?

JAMIE leaves.

He going to town?

CHICKY
He told you he was.

CLARENCE
Tell him I need him to pick me up something.

CHICKY
Jamie won't go to the liquor store for you now. You'll have to get your drinks over to the firehall.

CLARENCE takes the drawing out again.

CLARENCE
Remember how quick Trav learnt to ride a bike?

"Dad," he says to me. "Dad what are those wheels on to it?" "'Ems the training wheels Trav," I says to him. "Take them off, Dad, they're fucking stupid." Not a day over three years old, and riding a two-wheeler.

He looks good now don't he?

CHICKY
Jesus.
I don't know why you did that, Clarence, sent away for that artist rendition.
It's like you don't want that hurt to ever stop.
I want it to stop so bad.

She goes into the bedroom, slamming the door.

Lights out.

Scene 4

> *Sound of a car pulling up, door slamming, car peeling away.*

> *KEVIN, bawling like a calf, is heard outside.*

KEVIN
Jamie, Jamie, Jamie.

> *Loud thumping on the door. KEVIN staggers into the room, slightly illuminated by the porch light through the door. KEVIN is wearing a torn pair of underwear that he must hang on to, to keep from exposing himself. He stumbles around the kitchen knocking the chairs and collapses onto the floor.*

> *The kitchen light comes on. JAMIE stands in the doorway. He has just woken up and is wearing only his jeans.*

JAMIE
Jesus. *(Jesus.)*
Kev. Kev.
Jesus, you got the shit beat out of you.

> *CHICKY comes in.*

Get the door, Chicky.

CHICKY
Is he all right?

> *Throughout the scene, JAMIE handles KEVIN gently while verbally abusing him.*

JAMIE
Well, he ain't in very good shape.

> *KEVIN starts to throw up as JAMIE tenderly rolls him over on his side. CHICKY moves away from the stench.*

No blood in it, at least. He can't be bad inside.

> *KEVIN starts roaring like a bull calf and flailing his arms about.*

KEVIN
I'll kill you. I'll kill you, you. I'll kill you.

JAMIE
It's me, Jamie, you asshole.

> *CHICKY gets a bucket and cloth.*

KEVIN
Jamie... Jamie.

KEVIN throws up again.

CHICKY starts to clean up.

JAMIE
What do you think you're going to do?

CHICKY
Clean up.

JAMIE
He'll do that tomorrow when he's good and hung over.

KEVIN
Who's that, Jame?

CHICKY
It's me, Kev.

KEVIN
I'm sorry, Chicky. I'm sorry I'm sorry.

JAMIE
Yeah you'll be sorrier, too. Sit up.

KEVIN
My head hurts.

JAMIE
Come on, sit up. You ain't hurt so bad that I won't take a couple of swings at ya myself if you don't do as I say. *Sit the F up!*

KEVIN manages with help.

CHICKY
Who beat you, Kevin?

JAMIE
Merv, right?
I warned you, didn't I?
I should throw you out the goddamn door.
I should let you sleep in the goddamn manure pile tonight, where you belong.

CHICKY
How did he get out here?

JAMIE

Must have scared them.
Scared he was gonna choke on his own puke.
You got dropped off in the ditch like some useless piece of shit of
a dog.

CHICKY

Fuzzy, he's really hurting.

JAMIE

Help me get him up on the chair.

> *They manage to get him on a chair at the table. KEVIN lies with
> his head in his hands. CHICKY takes a blanket off the couch and
> wraps it around KEVIN.*

Go to bed, Chick.

CHICKY

Aren't you taking him to emergency?

JAMIE

No.

CHICKY

What if he's hurt inside?

JAMIE

I've seen a hell of a lot worse, and they didn't see no doctor.

CHICKY

Call the Mounties on Merv.

JAMIE

They won't do nothing.
You call the cops, next thing you know you'll be lookin' like this.

> *JAMIE gently lifts KEVIN'S head. His face is bruised and his
> mouth is bleeding.*

KEVIN

Chicky, I'm sorry… I threw up on your floor. I'm sorry.

CHICKY

It's okay, Kev. Are you okay? *(pause)* Kev?

KEVIN

I like you Chicky. I didn't mean to puke… look, look at that. Oh no.

JAMIE

He'll survive.

KEVIN

Oh God, I hate myself. I hate myself. I hate myself.

JAMIE

Go to bed, will you, so he'll shut up.

CHICKY leaves. JAMIE holds his face in his hands.

Let me look. Let's see your teeth. Jesus, you're some fucking lucky. Bet you've got some loose ones.

KEVIN

Jamie?

JAMIE uses a cloth to dab gently around his eyes and mouth. KEVIN shakes his head as if a thought has escaped him.

JAMIE

I told you, didn't I? I told you they just look for someone to get ugly at, didn't I?

KEVIN

I know you said. I know it.

JAMIE

That's right. Don't go to the camp with those guys, didn't I say?

KEVIN mumbles.

What? They said you was what?

KEVIN

I must be... I must be... if I never went then I must be... a bum boy.

JAMIE

They got what they wanted, didn't they? Merv got you up there.

KEVIN

They they they... was doing...

JAMIE

And that's what I told you.

KEVIN

They made me… they said if I didn't do it, they said they was gonna cut my balls up the… *(middle)* They made me… they made me…

KEVIN starts to bawl.

JAMIE

I don't want to hear what those pervs made you do. You keep that goddamn stuff to yourself. You hear me?

KEVIN nods holding his head.

Don't tell nobody. Nobody.

KEVIN

Make those fuckers pay.

JAMIE

You went swimming with the alligators.

KEVIN

Make those fuckers pay.

JAMIE

It was your own goddamn stupid fault. When your eyes is better, when every last bit of blue and green and yellow's all gone, I'm going to punch them black and blue to teach you a lesson.

KEVIN moans.

You can sleep in Clarence's chair, it cleans up easier.

JAMIE guides him to the chair and settles him in. He notices the manila envelope and opens it staring intently at the artist rendition.

KEVIN

I'm sorry, Jamie.

JAMIE turns the picture over and reads the back. He puts it back.

I'm sorry, Jamie.

JAMIE

F— sorry, Kev.
Merv's got nothing to do except truck pulp and think up trouble. I'm telling ya something now because you ain't going to remember what I've told you tomorrow.

KEVIN is half-awake through this.

KEVIN

I'll 'member, Jame.

JAMIE

No you won't.
Unless you've got *extend the memory* for alcohol blackouts.
I don't want you to remember what I'm telling ya anyway because this is something you have to figure out for yourself. You got to take Merv on now. YOU. Because if I have to help you, Merv's gonna have your balls forever.

KEVIN

No no no no.

JAMIE

Don't you bawl. Go to sleep.

JAMIE starts to go back to bed.

KEVIN

Jame. They was talking about your stag. They gonna get you drunked up and dress you up in women's clothes. They was saying they're all going to bring bras and stuff. Merv gonna bring a maxi-pad he said, to stuff down your panties. After you pass out he gonna take you into town and leave you in the Tim Horton's parking lot dressed like that.

JAMIE

Okay, Kev. Good thing you told me.

KEVIN

Good on me, eh, Jamie? *(He beams, laughing through smashed lips.)*

JAMIE

Good on you, bud.
Sleep it all off.

JAMIE leaves.

Lights out.

Scene 5

Midnight, Sunday night. CLARENCE sits in the chair staring at the television screen. The head and shoulders of Travis are on the screen but move in a whirling motion.

CLARENCE

Stop doing that now… stop moving for *Chrissakes*. I got to talk to you. There's this place in Scotland, where they got it now that they can clone people. Don't matter how long you've been dead, alls they need is a chip of your bone to get your DNA and they can make you all over again. I've been thinking if we took one of Chicky's eggs and DNA from you… well that's the thing ya got to let me do the thing… ya got to not care about it so you'll be born again. The government's doing it now. The USA government has Johnny and Robbie Kennedy living little kids now, but they'll be back. Then you'll see. There will be resurrections, just like that Bible picture you loved, of people out of their graves, looking cured of dirt-bike accidents, and cancers and, well, not AIDS, they'll make a rule about that, but you'll be born again. I'll live to see that, Trav, I'll live to see that, by God.

The sound of CHICKY and KRISTA arriving.

They are "shhhhhing."

CLARENCE swallows his drink and scrunches down in his chair like he is sleeping. CHICKY comes in with KRISTA. KRISTA is wearing a shower hat made out of a paper plate with all the ribbons and bows attached from the gifts she opened.

KRISTA stops at the door, noting that the TV is on, and gestures at CHICKY that she won't come in. CHICKY walks over to the TV, turns it off.

CHICKY

He's dead to the world.

KRISTA

He'll wake up if he hears me.

CHICKY holds up an empty rum bottle.

CHICKY

Not sleeping… passed out.

KRISTA
> You going to put him to bed?

CHICKY
> *(Gross.)* Not likely.
> Take that stupid thing off.

KRISTA
> I like wearing it.
> I was totally surprised.
> When they all shouted *surprise*, I almost pissed myself.

CHICKY
> I thought you had guessed.

KRISTA
> No, I swear.
> I was so mad when Carol said that.
> Who invited her?

CHICKY
> It was an open shower.

KRISTA
> She just came to say it.

CHICKY
> *(tired)* Yeah, Carol's a bitch.

KRISTA
> If I was you, I'd get pregnant, too.

CHICKY
> Right.

KRISTA
> Reg would have to leave her then.

CHICKY
> Why?

KRISTA
> I mean he would want to. He must want you to have his babies.
> I want to have Jamie's. Don't you want to have his babies?

CHICKY
> I haven't used birth control since I was sixteen.
> He might have left her back then, if I had got knocked up.

KRISTA
I hate that expression.

CHICKY laughs.

She is such a cow.

CHICKY laughs.

What are you gonna say when you see him?

CHICKY
Congratulations.

KRISTA
Maybe you should see a doctor.

CHICKY
What for?

KRISTA
Maybe you just got to have some little operation like Mom did. Get your tubes flushed? Well it worked for Mom. She tried to have kids for ten years. She got her tubes flushed, and then Kevin and me came one, two, like that.

CHICKY
Anyway, I know why I can't have his baby.

KRISTA
Why?

CHICKY
God's saying to me, "You're screwing another woman's husband. I will not allow his seed to grow in your womb."

KRISTA
If God had that rule, your mother never would have had you.

CHICKY
What do you know about it?

KRISTA
Nothing. I heard he was a married man, is all.

CHICKY
Did you "heard" who the married man was?

KRISTA

Nobody knows, do they? Sorry. Anyway "*God saying*," that's weird holy-roller stuff. You don't even go to church.

CHICKY

This has nothing to do with the church, this is about the balance of… I don't know. When I lay down in my bed at night, and I put my hand here, I can feel Reg's sperm running under my fingers… like lamprey eels running up the river. Me not having a baby seems like the way of the world, or something.
Like the world has rules.
Like because of what Mom did to Trav, she caused his cancer.

KRISTA

Nobody can cause a brain tumour.

CHICKY

When she left us he was three years old. The doctor said that tumour started when he was three years old. Maybe when she told him the first time, she told him she was going to come and get him, she said those words, "I'll get you next week, Trav," and then she didn't. Well *those words* were inside his head with no place to go, so they seeded in his brain, a spore of a tumour started, and got fed all those years with her broken promises until Trav was nine years old and it was incurable.

KRISTA

Carol being pregnant has got you down, Chicky, you don't think that.

CHICKY

A tumour grew inside his brain and he died.
When Jamie goes on about retards and homosexuals, I think God's going to make one of your children retarded or gay… Jame boy. See if he doesn't.

KRISTA

That's a nice thing to say. They'll be my kids too.

CHICKY

Don't marry him.

KRISTA

What?

CHICKY
> I'm serious.

KRISTA
> We just came from my wedding shower that *you* put on for me.

CHICKY
> You want the wedding, the dress, the scroll tied with a fuchsia ribbon.
> You want to see the teachers' faces when you walk into graduation with a gold band on your finger.
> But do you want Jamie?

KRISTA
> I'm marrying him, aren't I?

CHICKY
> He can be so hard. You've seen him be hard. He's getting worse.

KRISTA
> He won't be like that when he's happy.

CHICKY
> With you?

KRISTA
> He wants to marry me.

CHICKY
> Why?

KRISTA
> Because. I. Love. Him. Your mother never did. His father goes on and on about Travis Travis Travis as if Jamie was never born. I guess because he's marrying me, now his sister hates him too.

CHICKY
> Sister? I've been his *mother*, even before Mom left us, since I was five years old I was his mother. I carried him, I fed him, I held him, I kissed his little peach-fuzz head when he cried, me. *(pause)* I was his mother.

KRISTA
> You're jealous then, because he's leaving you.

CHICKY

I want him to leave. I want him to go somewhere, anywhere far away. If he marries you, he'll never leave.

KRISTA

Why should he? He's got a job here.

CHICKY

He's told Earl he's quitting.

KRISTA

(pause, recovers) He'll hire him back, he always does.

CHICKY

But Jamie hates the work.

KRISTA

He's got to stop thinking about it is all. The pay is good. We want to build right away.

CHICKY

Would you go with him if he got work someplace else?

KRISTA

We don't have land someplace else, we got land here. We're going to start building soon. It's going to be the house of the village.

CHICKY

Wait one year. Have the wedding next year.

KRISTA

That's a great thing for my maid of honour to say. Everything is set, ready.

God, well don't be my maid of honour if that's how you feel.

CHICKY

Okay. I won't.

KRISTA

What? You're some *(pause)* witch aren't you?

She walks out. CLARENCE stirs as though waking up.

CHICKY

Get your ears full?

Lights out.

Scene 6

> *This is Monday, the night of the stag. JAMIE and KEVIN sit at the*
> *kitchen table. JAMIE has on nylons, a bright skirt and a T-shirt*
> *over a size DD bra that is stuffed to the max. KEVIN is putting*
> *on makeup in a makeup mirror. KEVIN is also supposed to be*
> *getting dressed up, but he seems to be avoiding it. JAMIE has to*
> *nudge him on. They are both nursing beers. CLARENCE sits in his*
> *chair flicking channels.*

KEVIN

It's got to hurt, man.

JAMIE

It don't hurt.

KEVIN

Smacking the water like that.

JAMIE

If you do it right, you don't feel a fucking thing.

KEVIN

I did it from the rail. It hurt.

JAMIE

The rail's for pansies. You do it from the top frame.
You make sure you're dead centre in that hole, too, or you're dead.
Ha.
When you do it right it's smooth.

KEVIN

When you're drunk out of your gourd!

JAMIE

Yeah. *(laughs)*
I'll show you how, Kev. It'll get the chest hairs growing onto you.

KEVIN

Krista says you can't do it anymore when you're married.

JAMIE

If Krista told me *not* to jump off a bridge, wouldn't I?

> *KRISTA comes in at that moment. She reacts instantly to the*
> *scene.*

KRISTA

Oh my God. Jamie! Kevin. You guys. You're not really going like that are you?

JAMIE

A little surprise for Merv, right, Kev?

JAMIE moves in on her.

KRISTA

You got lip gloss on me. *Yuck,* watermelon. I hate that stuff. Did you get the washing machine?

JAMIE

I got it, but it's a piece of shit.

KRISTA

No it isn't.

JAMIE

They don't know how to take care of nothing.

KRISTA

It is only two years old. It doesn't have a scratch on it.

KEVIN laughs.

What are you laughing at?

JAMIE

He agrees with me.

KRISTA

Where is it?

JAMIE

In the shed.

KRISTA goes out.

KEVIN

You're dead meat now.

JAMIE

More eye shadow, Kev.

JAMIE pushes a pink satin dress in KEVIN's direction.

KEVIN

I don't know if I can do this, man.

JAMIE
  Pink's your colour, Kev.

  KEVIN takes the dress.

  We'll show those bastards not to fuck with… *(us)*

  KRISTA bursts in.

KRISTA
  What did you do to it?

JAMIE
  I didn't do nothing to it.

KRISTA
  Well somebody beat on it with a hammer or an axe or something. *Kevin?*

KEVIN
  I never touched it. Well, I put it on the back of the truck.

KRISTA
  You never bought it like that. What happened?

KEVIN
  It fell off the truck.

KRISTA
  You didn't tie it on?

JAMIE
  Nope.

KEVIN
  We was only goin' from there to here.

JAMIE
  If Merv hadn't cut me off, it wouldn't have fallen off.

KEVIN
  Merv passed him.

JAMIE
  Cut me off.

KEVIN
  Yeah. When Jamie pulled out to pass him, it fell off.

We didn't notice 'til we got here. Some lucky it slid off onto the side, nobody ran into it.

JAMIE

I wish it *would have* hit Merv.

KRISTA

You had to pass him.

JAMIE

Yes I had to pass him. The shit.
I told you we don't need a washer anyway.

KRISTA

How am I suppose to do our laundry?

JAMIE

At your mother's.

KRISTA

Mom won't help us, she's told us that.

CLARENCE

In my day people didn't expect to have everything when they got married. They was willing to wait for things.

KRISTA

Oh   my   God. I told you.

JAMIE

No one asked you.

CLARENCE

I was only saying.

KRISTA

I *told* you.
This is what I've been *saying.*

JAMIE

Stay the fuck out of our business.

CLARENCE

I was only saying.

JAMIE

Don't.

KRISTA

That's a hundred and fifty dollars gone.

KRISTA takes out a sheet of paper and a book. She works at her homework at the table. The guys continue getting decked out for the stag.

Jesus.
I hate poetry.

JAMIE

Hey, don't you swear.

KRISTA

Jeepers, I hate poetry.

JAMIE

Too bad, because you're marrying a poet.

KEVIN laughs.

Two lips are red
Nipples are pink
Farts in a bed
Sure do stink.

JAMIE takes a bow.

KRISTA

I told Mr. Dagly I don't have time to do an essay. I told him I'm getting married on Saturday. He said, "I know, Krista, your colour scheme is the talk of the school." He said he overheard two guys in the locker room, like, discussing how relieved they were that I had gone with fuchsia, because it was so much more June bride than winter mint.

JAMIE

He's a fag.

KRISTA

You don't have to say that every time.
Every time I mention Dagly you say that.

JAMIE

"Fagly."

KRISTA

I have to do the essay, or I fail English.

JAMIE
> You're not failing.

KRISTA
> I know.

JAMIE
> I'm telling you *you're not failing.*

KRISTA
> I said *I know.*
> I don't care if I don't pass.

JAMIE
> You're getting your grade twelve if it takes you twenty years.
> Read the poem. Kev'll tell you what it's about.

KRISTA
> Yeah, right.

KEVIN
> You know I'm smarter than you, sister.

KRISTA
> *(reading)* "Bird Cage.
> I am a bird cage
> A cage of bone
> With a bird
>
> The bird in the cage of bone
> Is death building his nest
>
> When nothing is happening
> One can hear him ruffle his wings.
>
> And when one has laughed a lot
> If one suddenly stops
> One hears him cooing
> Far down
> Like a small bell.
>
> It is a bird held captive
> This death in my cage of bone
>
> Would he not like to fly away
> Is it you who will hold him back

Is it I
What is it

He cannot fly away
Until he has eaten all
My heart
The source of blood
With my life inside

He will have my soul in his beak."

> *JAMIE has lost his smirk and he seems drawn into the poem.*
> *KEVIN breaks the mood.*

KEVIN
Jesus. Well he is talking about his bird so I guess he's talking about his... *(He grabs his crotch.)* Eh, Jame?

KRISTA
Thank you, Kevin. Jesus. *Jeepers.*
The guy was dying. He had a heart something, so he knew he was dying. I have to write an essay describing my personal *bird of death*.

JAMIE
Death would be cancer or something. You're not dying.

KRISTA
Dagly told me to write how a marriage is a cage and a husband is the bird of death. I told him I'm not doing that.

JAMIE
The fag.

> *JAMIE and KEVIN start a small chorus of "fag, fag fag" – like bullfrogs sounding off in a pond.*

KRISTA
I can't get anything done here. I'm going home. Call me after the stag, Jamie. Jamie? Call me.
There was this article in the *Wedding Digest* and this girl's boyfriend died at his stag. Alcohol poisoning. You know Merv will get you too drunk.

JAMIE
The bird of death... alcohol – the bird of paradise, alcohol.

KEVIN

I'll drink to that. And may it fly up my nose.

KRISTA

Call me.

> *KRISTA leaves.*

JAMIE

Well, Kev buddy, get your dress on and let's go fuck with Merv.

> *Lights out.*

Scene 7

> *At the river. Wednesday suppertime. CHICKY is waiting, checking her watch. While she has her back turned, ROBBY comes down.*

ROBBY

Hi, Chicky.

CHICKY

Hey, Robby.

ROBBY

How are you?

CHICKY

I feel used up and spit out.
I feel like I've been fifty years old since I was three.

ROBBY

(pause) How are you?

CHICKY

Good. How are you?

ROBBY

Good.

CHICKY

Was Reg at the farm when you left?

ROBBY

No. Reg and Carol went to town in the Ford truck.

> *CHICKY realizes REG is not coming.*

(*emphatically*) I'm done working for Reg.

CHICKY

Are you?

ROBBY

(*emphatically*) He said he don't need me no more.

CHICKY

You don't need Reg. I don't need Reg.
We don't need Reg.

ROBBY

We don't need Reg.

CHICKY

This is your chance, Robby. You can go anywhere in the world.
Take a plane anywhere.

ROBBY

I don't like planes.

CHICKY

It's better to drive, anyway. You see everything then.
Tell me where you want to go?

ROBBY

Don't know.

CHICKY

Some place you saw on TV. How about that?

ROBBY

Don't know.

CHICKY

You've been thinking about going away.

ROBBY

No.

CHICKY

Now you can.

ROBBY

No.

CHICKY

Paris, France.

ROBBY

French people there.

CHICKY

Australia… New York.

You going to ask me to come, too?

ROBBY

Okay.

No.

CHICKY

Robby and Donalda on the road.

ROBBY

Mom says no.

CHICKY

We'll bring her.

ROBBY

Mom has to stay with Lissa.

CHICKY

Bring Lissa, okay.

Got any money saved up?

I know you didn't think this would happen. I know you thought I'm going to live here all my life. And something important, not important, some miracle was going to happen and it was going to all work out, but now you need money, did you save up?

ROBBY

No.

CHICKY

Me neither. That's what happens when you're stupid.

Oh, Robby. I'm stupid. Me me I'm stupid. Stupid.

ROBBY

No you're smart, you passed me at school.

CHICKY

I'm stupid at life.

I'm Reg stupid.

ROBBY

(*laughs*) Donalda?

CHICKY

> That's right. See we're already on our way.

ROBBY

> Got to hay for Reg tomorrow.
> Reg said, "See you tomorrow."

CHICKY

> You said you were all done working for Reg.

ROBBY

> Yup. Five o'clock all done, don't need me no more.
> Tomorrow morning at ten. Haying.

CHICKY

> I'm not going back, Robby.
> I'm not going back.
> I'm already half gone.

ROBBY

> Supper now, got to go home for supper. You going now, Chicky?

CHICKY

> Nope.

ROBBY

> Bye, Chicky.

> *ROBBY leaves.*

> *KEVIN steps into view up on the road. He swings his legs over the rail, like he is getting set to jump.*

KEVIN

> Hey, Chicky.

CHICKY

> How long have you been up there?

KEVIN

> "I feel used up and spit out."

CHICKY

> What are you doing up there, anyway?

KEVIN

> Jumping.

CHICKY
Why are you in such a hurry to mess yourself up?

KEVIN comes down.

You still look bad.

KEVIN
Old Merv thinks we're done. I'm not done with him.

CHICKY
Remember, his wife calls the cops.
You not working today?

KEVIN
Nope. Been up to the Curl Hole.

CHICKY
Power company drained it, did they?

KEVIN
(nods) I'll get some nice white pine out of there.

CHICKY
Why didn't they log it before they built the dam?

KEVIN
Don't know but lucky for me. Fifteen years underwater, man that wood's gonna be pretty when it's polished up.

CHICKY
You get Jamie's and Krista's table finished?

KEVIN
Yeah. Made you something, too.

CHICKY
What?

KEVIN takes something out of his pocket.

KEVIN
You got to come over here to see it, don't ya?

CHICKY comes forward and puts her hand out.

Well you got to give me a kiss first, don't ya!

CHICKY
No.

KEVIN tries to kiss her.

Kevin stop.

CHICKY takes the small object from his hand.

A baby porcupine, sleeping.

KEVIN
(sullen) Maybe it's road kill.

CHICKY
Kev. You are so good at this.

KEVIN
Not good enough for a kiss.

CHICKY brushes his cheek with her lips.

Come on, Chicky a real kiss…

KEVIN tries to kiss her.

CHICKY
Kev, your face. I don't think you're up to much… especially that.

KEVIN overreacts.

KEVIN
What does that mean? What are they saying? What are those bastards saying about me?

KEVIN moves to put his arms around her.

CHICKY
Kevin, no! We're not… kissing cousins, okay.

KEVIN
We're not gonna be cousins, we will be in-laws… outlaws.

CHICKY ignores him.

I'll go away with you.

CHICKY
Where would I go?

KEVIN moves to kiss her again.

Jesus. Leave me alone.

KEVIN persists.

Keep your hands off me.
No. No!
You touch me again and I am telling Reg.
Shit.

> *CHICKY throws the carved porcupine back at him and leaves.*

KEVIN
I'm sorry, here take it. I made it for you.

> *But CHICKY is gone.*

Chicky, I'm sorry.
You slow danced with me.
Merv and them are lying.
I never did what they said I did.

> *KEVIN sits on the sand. He hits himself on the bruises. He is near tears.*

I could do it with you, Chicky.
I could do it with you.

> *Above, LISSA, a plump girl of fourteen, comes out onto the bridge. She is humming "Happy Birthday" and carrying a colourful umbrella. She stops and looks down at KEVIN.*

LISSA
Is my brother Robby here?

KEVIN
Do you see him?

> *KEVIN pulls himself together. She comes down calling.*

LISSA
Robby? Robby, Robby, Robby.

KEVIN
He ain't here. He left.

LISSA
He's got to come home for supper.
It's his birthday.
Mom got a bucket of chicken.
Sarah Lee cake.
You hurt yourself?

KEVIN
Yeah it looks that way.

LISSA
(*importantly*) Yeah, it looks that way.

KEVIN
How come you got that umbrella? It's not raining.

LISSA
Nope.

KEVIN
So how come you got it then?

LISSA
Mom got it in town.

KEVIN
Don't touch my eye.

LISSA
Does it hurt?

KEVIN
Yes it hurts.

LISSA
Mom kisses hurts.

> *KEVIN studies her a long moment. She gives his eye a quick kiss.*

KEVIN
It feels better but it hurts right here.

> *LISSA kisses his cheek.*

Now it hurts right there.

> *LISSA, giggling, kisses his other cheek quickly – shyly.*

Didn't work that time.

> *LISSA kisses him with more intent.*

You got it.
You got any hurts.

> *LISSA holds out the back of her hand.*

LISSA
Cat scratched me, Keving.

KEVIN
I see that.

> *KEVIN kisses her hand very gently. LISSA smiles and brings her hand back.*

I hurt under here too.

> *KEVIN points to under his T-shirt.*

I can't even see all my hurts back there.
Do I got any?

> *KEVIN slips his T-shirt off. LISSA looks shyly, then begins to kiss his back in little flutters. She is so childlike.*

LISSA
All done.

KEVIN
But now you got all my hurts on your lips.

> *KEVIN reaches for her and starts to pull her mouth towards his. This is still a game to LISSA. KEVIN lays her down and moves to kiss her. At that moment KEVIN realizes what he is doing is wrong, and he pulls on his T-shirt.*

You better get home, Lissa.
Robby'll be waiting for his birthday supper.

LISSA
Don't want to.

KEVIN
You'll miss the birthday cake.

LISSA
Don't care.

KEVIN
And the present opening.

LISSA
(darkly) Robby's presents.

KEVIN

You want a present?

LISSA

Mom says, "Not *your* birthday, missy."

KEVIN

If I give you a present, will you go home?

LISSA

Don't know.

KEVIN

Okay. Too bad, it's a nice present.

LISSA

Okay okay okay!

> *KEVIN turns around and closes his hands around the little porcupine. He turns back.*

KEVIN

Okay, open my hands.

LISSA

That's not a present with *Happy Birthday!* paper.

KEVIN

It's better. It's harder to open.

> *LISSA half tries, but in the end he makes her work to get his hands apart.*

LISSA

Oh, a porcupine. It's dead.

KEVIN

No. It's asleep.

LISSA

That's okay, it's not dead, it's asleep. It's mine, right Keving?

KEVIN

Yeah.

> *Before he is aware of what she is up to, she kisses him on the lips hard.*

Lissa! Don't kiss me 'cause I give you something.

LISSA

(*sulking*) I want to, Keving.

KEVIN

(*angry at her innocence*) No you don't! Go home, now.

LISSA

Bye, Keving.

LISSA hurries away. KEVIN sits with his head in his hands.

Lights down.

Scene 8

Early Wednesday evening. JAMIE sits in CLARENCE's chair with the phone in his lap. He gets up, goes and gets a beer, and comes back to the phone. He dials a long distance number. The audience does not hear the voice on the other end of the call, but the lines are included within square brackets to help the actor give his lines the proper weight.

JAMIE

[GCT Flight School, Janet speaking.] Yeah, hello, I'm calling to… [Can you hold the line please?] Yeah, sure.

JAMIE paces around waiting to be taken off hold.

Yeah, hi, I'm calling about the ad you ran in the paper out here. [Where are you calling from, sir?] Nova Scotia. [Oh, those ads, we ran them several months ago.] Yeah I guess it's been a couple of months. Anyway, I am very interested in joining your heli-logging team. [What position?] Pilot. [You are a pilot?] No, *training*, sorry, *training* to be a pilot… you know, be the one that flies the trees out. I'm experienced in the woods. [Yes?] Yeah, I've worked the processor for four years. [Chainsaw trained?] I've worked chainsaw, but I'm looking to, you know, do the helicopter training. [We've met our training quota for this training period.] Oh, so when is the next training session. [April if we have enough trainees sign up.] Nothing before like, next April? Okay, could you put my name on the waiting list now? [Well maybe I should tell you the requirements and costs.] Yeah, sure. [You want to write this down?] Yeah, I got a pen and paper and everything, go ahead.

*JAMIE sneaks a swig of beer. He doesn't write any of the
information down.*

[The course can take up to five months.] I am interested in the
three-month course. [If you want to be able to fly at night…] Yeah,
Jesus, five months, okay. I do want to be able to fly at night. [The
cost is forty thousand dollars.] Four thousand [Forty.] no, I was
joking you, I knew you said forty… thousand. [And we'll need
a medical and high school graduation certificate.] Right, medical
sure… listen, I got a buddy who is interested in doing training too,
but… he's real experienced in the woods too. He, the guy, didn't
graduate from high school but he's getting, I mean he's got the GED
thing. [Well he would have to take an entrance test make sure his
math was up to speed.] Yeah, sure I'll tell him about that test you
know, 'cause he needs to know if his math is, like you said, up to
speed. Thanks now. [Should I take your name.] No… no I won't
leave my name.

JAMIE hangs up.

Fuck you, lady.
(quietly) Fuck *me.*

Lights down.

Scene 9

*It is 2 a.m. on Thursday morning. The river scene is lit by a street
lamp mounted on the bridge. CLARENCE comes down to the
beach. His clothes are covered in dirt, which he is attempting
to brush off. He begins to wash his hands in the water. He is
throbbing with excitement. He stops, calming himself. He reaches
into his hunting vest and takes out a square of cloth. CLARENCE
carefully unwraps it and cradles the small bone in his hand.*

CLARENCE
You'll see you'll see you'll see.
I did it for you.
That's all I want.

JAMIE
Clarence.
This is God.

JAMIE sits in his usual spot on the rail nursing his fifth beer – the empties are lined up beside him. JAMIE burps loudly.

CLARENCE
Jesus, Jamie, Christ—

JAMIE
That's me.

CLARENCE
You scared the shit out of me.

CLARENCE wraps up the bone quickly and puts it back in his vest.

JAMIE
(laughs) What have you got there?

CLARENCE
Nothing.

JAMIE
You've got *something*, you put *something* in your pocket.

CLARENCE
I ain't got nothing.

He washes his hands again.

JAMIE
What are you *doing* down there, washing your hands?

CLARENCE
I ain't doing nothing no worse than you.

JAMIE
Ah ah ah, remember Oprah. Talk to your kids.

CLARENCE
A man can come down to the river.

JAMIE
At 2:30 in the morning?

CLARENCE
You're here. What are you doing?

JAMIE
Thinking about going for a swim.

CLARENCE
The lamprey ain't left the river yet.

JAMIE
I don't see any eels.

CLARENCE
I don't need to see them, I know they're there. It hasn't thundered and lightninged yet.

JAMIE
What do they do, Clarence? *Holy shit*, it's thundering and lightning out there boys, time to wiggle our asses out of here so folks can swim.

CLARENCE
It kills them off. The old people know that.

JAMIE
You got all the answers, don't ya, Clarence?

> *JAMIE comes down to stand beside CLARENCE. JAMIE invades CLARENCE's space, forcing him to move back and step around JAMIE's building rage.*

Well here's a question for ya.
What was I going to be when I grew up?

CLARENCE
Trav was gonna be a soldier.

JAMIE
Yeah yeah "in the Airborne" and I was gonna be…?

CLARENCE
I remember you telling us you was going to be an astronaut, only you said astrosnot.

JAMIE
That's because I was fucking four years old. What did I want to be when I was sixteen? When I quit school, what was I quitting I was gonna be?

CLARENCE
You never said.

JAMIE

I brought the information home from the guidance counsellor... set
it right on the goddamn kitchen table.

CLARENCE

That was years ago.

JAMIE

Found out you let them put me in the retarded math.

CLARENCE

No, Chicky told you it was non-uni (...*versity prep*).

JAMIE

Retarded. Retarded to pilot school. You let those teachers screw me.

CLARENCE

They never told me nothing.

JAMIE

No you were too fucking stupid to ask.
Where are you going?

CLARENCE

I'm leaving. It's a free country. You think you can blame everything
on to me. My fox farm failed because of fucking Bridget fucking
Bardot, my wife left me, my son died... he *died*. What was
I supposed to do when those teachers told me, "Put Jamie in
this math class and he'll get better marks." Eh? I was a broken
man, what in hell was I supposed to do?

CLARENCE leaves.

*JAMIE climbs up on "the high," on top of the bridge frame. He
stands, swinging his arms as though warming up to jump.*

Lights down.

ACT II

Scene 10

Thursday morning. KRISTA sits at the table writing out thank-you notes. JAMIE comes in carrying a beer and three partridge eggs.

KRISTA

Ten more for you to sign.
I'm not bringing them shower gifts into this house.
I'll keep them at home 'til we move to the trailer.
Same with the wedding ones too.

JAMIE puts the eggs on the table. She touches the eggs.

They're cold.
What's a hen supposed to do with partridge babies anyway?
You shouldn't do that. Walk around looking for them after your shift.

JAMIE

You hear them when you get out of the machine.

KRISTA

You can't hear eggs.

JAMIE

Jesus, I hear their mothers looking for their nests, looking for their babies.

KRISTA

I know you can't hear eggs. I was kidding, Fuzzy.

JAMIE

I told you, don't call me that.

KRISTA

Chicky does. The men at the firehall all do.

JAMIE

I don't want you to.

KRISTA

That's not fair.

JAMIE

Come here.

JAMIE kisses her and whispers something in her ear. She looks at him.

KRISTA

What do you mean?

JAMIE

Mom said "Jamieeee" like "What are you up to, you little shit."
Clarence says Jamie like "not Travis," the one he wants alive. Like,
"*NotTravis*, you going to the liquor store today?"

> *KRISTA crawls onto his lap. Kisses him on the mouth.*

And when the teachers said "Jamie," well, weren't they thinking
Dumb ass?

KRISTA

Jamie, stop—

JAMIE

There.

KRISTA

What?

JAMIE

Even when you are *pissed* at me. There's something – you say Jamie
like there's a chance of something… in me.

KRISTA

Jamie jamie jamie jamie jamie…

> *They kiss.*

Want to?

JAMIE

I'm saving myself 'til I'm married.
I can wait.

> *KRISTA kisses him.*

I might have to take a trip to the vet before supper.
The eagle's not looking too good.
He's losing feathers. His eyes look milky.

KRISTA

Half what you rescue dies.
Like that baby raccoon that time.

Like those eggs.
Is that why you're quitting? Chicky told me.

> *JAMIE speaks his line to the bedroom door, indicating that he knows she is in there.*

JAMIE
Sis needs to keep her nose out of my business.

KRISTA
It's my business. I'm marrying you the day after tomorrow.

JAMIE
I don't work chainsaw.

KRISTA
That don't make sense. You hate what the processor does but you won't work chainsaw. You got to have a job.

JAMIE
That's the thing, Krista, in ten years there won't be logging jobs around here.
The woods is tapped out. In ten years, *less* even, there won't be any trees in this valley.

KRISTA
What are you talking about? It's woods all the way to town and that's over forty miles.

JAMIE
You don't know what you're looking at. All along the roads is not woods anymore. What you're seeing is a screen of trees two, three tier deep and behind that hectares and hectares of clear cut. Everything has been chewed up and spit out. Not one tree standing. That's why.... Listen, Krista, I'm not saying we can afford to do this right away but I'm thinking—

> *KEVIN burst in.*

KEVIN
Where's Clarence?

JAMIE
Jesus, Kevin, what's crawled up your ass?

KEVIN
Is he here? Where is he?

CHICKY comes out of the bedroom.

Chicky, where's Clarence?

CHICKY

It's the colostomy clinic day at the hospital.

JAMIE

The fun never stops for old Clarence.

KEVIN

Good, good, 'cause if he hears this, he's gonna to have a stroke or something.

CHICKY

Kevin, what are you talking about?

KEVIN

They're burying Betty's boy tomorrow, right?

CHICKY

I told him not to call Betty again. He's telling them to send the body to Florida to be frozen.

KEVIN

No, Chicky, Ronnie went over to check the grave site and he saw. They've been fucking with Trav's grave.

CHICKY

Who has?

JAMIE

What did you have to tell her for, Kev? Jesus.

CHICKY

Fuzzy, what's he talking about?

JAMIE

It's okay, Chicky. I've taken care of it. I'm getting sod from Reg.

CHICKY

Sod, for what?

JAMIE

It was probably some animal digging around. Forget it.

KEVIN

Ronnie says it weren't no animal. They like dug a big hole straight down the middle of the plot – got Betty all upset. Fucking Merv.

CHICKY
Why would he bother Trav's grave?

KEVIN
Someone laid a beating onto him at Jamie's stag so he's paying him back.

CHICKY
Jamie.

JAMIE
Do you see a mark on me?

KEVIN
Don't blame Jamie, we was only getting back at Merv for what he did to me.

CHICKY
This has gone far enough, Kevin.
Merv's got kids.

KEVIN
He don't act like it. If you got kids you don't dig up some other kid's grave.

JAMIE
No – not some other kid's grave.
Kev. Go get the sod from Reg, okay?

KEVIN
What about Merv?

CHICKY
You don't know that it was him.

KEVIN
You kidding? You tell her, Jamie.

JAMIE
Maybe it wasn't.

KEVIN
Jamie, he did it, I know it, you know it.

JAMIE
I'll meet you at the grave – make it look like nothing happened there for Betty tomorrow.

KEVIN

Let me, Jamie. I'll fix it up right.
Then I'm going to go get that son of a bitch.

KEVIN leaves. CHICKY looks at KRISTA.

CHICKY

Are you going to do something?

KRISTA

What? Besides Merv... he started it, right?
Kevin will be a mess in the wedding photos.

CHICKY

I don't care about your *(fucking)* wedding pictures.

KRISTA

See, Jamie? Make her stop ruining our wedding.
Well?
I'm going home.

KRISTA seems to expect JAMIE to go with her.

I said I'm going home.

KRISTA leaves clearly angry.

CHICKY

I don't think even Merv would do something like that.

JAMIE

It don't matter to Kevin who did it.
He needs for it to be Merv.

CHICKY

Why?

JAMIE

Look, Chicky. Merv did something to Kev, Kev's got to take Merv on.
If he wants to live around here anyway.

CHICKY

What did he do to Kev to make him so crazy?

JAMIE

I don't ask what Merv the perv does. You saw him. They got him
good and drunk that's for sure. Maybe they fed him some Viagra,
made him look at someone's dick and told him if his pecker got hard

it meant he's a queer. Anyway, you know they got his underwear off him one way or another.

CHICKY
He's acting like he's going to kill Merv.

JAMIE
If Kevin got laid, sis, he'd be all right.

CHICKY
You know he might be the same to me as you.

JAMIE
You're putting a lot of faith in shit Mom told you.

CHICKY
You tell Kev, that's enough.

JAMIE
I'll tell, don't mean he'll listen.

CHICKY
When are you going to B.C.?

JAMIE
Soon enough.

CHICKY
Not soon enough.
You've had that ad for months.
Have you called?

JAMIE
That ain't your business, but yes I did.

CHICKY
So you are going?

JAMIE
Soon as I get the money together.

CHICKY
You *quit* your job.

JAMIE
Danny's renting the trailer 'til spring. We'll have enough to move out there by then.

CHICKY
You might have the wedding paid off by then.
Why are you marrying her? It's not like you're lovesick.

JAMIE
Now you sound like her. "Do you love me? Do you really really love me"? Fuuuuuuuuuuuuuuuuuuuucccccccccccckkkkkkk.

CHICKY
She'll stop you from going.

JAMIE
No she won't. Krista's going too.

CHICKY
You'd do better on your own.

JAMIE
I need one person with me who knows me.

CHICKY
You marry her, you'll be stuck.
She'll get pregnant…

JAMIE
No, we ain't having kids for a long time.

CHICKY
You're being a stupid married man, and you're not even married.

JAMIE
Yeah, I heard Carol's preggers.

CHICKY
Yeah, well, so I know what I'm talking about.

JAMIE
You know, sis, old Reggie's using you up, same as he's using up the interval land. What are *you* sticking around for?

CHICKY
Haven't you noticed I've been taking care of you?

JAMIE
So now you don't have to. And don't wait around here for some someday family reunion. Mom probably doesn't know who your father is, for sure.

CHICKY
I can't stand living with you sometimes.

JAMIE
I'm not saying anything against you. It's her I'm talking about.

CHICKY
You used to have a heart. You used to have feelings.

JAMIE
Yeah?

CHICKY
You weren't like this before.

JAMIE
Before when?

CHICKY
I don't know. Before Travis died. Before you quit school.
Before you started drinking every day.

JAMIE
You know what I feel these days?

CHICKY
What?

JAMIE
(pause) Nothing.

CHICKY
No… tell me.

JAMIE
Nothing is what I feel after a twelve-hour night shift shaking inside
that machine. Hearing everything outside it get tore up. The men say
don't walk around a section you've just clear cut. Earl and them say
if it makes you feel bad don't do it. I can't just walk away… leave
things half-dead and dying.

CHICKY
Is that why you're drinking, causing trouble with Merv?

JAMIE
Merv isn't anything. All that is just… something stupid to do.
What makes you feel better after a sunny afternoon of stripping the
top soil off interval land?

CHICKY
I certainly don't go beating up people.

JAMIE
Have you looked at Reg's wife lately? Carol looks like you've given her a bruising more than once.

CHICKY
Jesus.

JAMIE
And you're worried about what I'm doing to Merv's kids?

CHICKY
Jesus you've got some nerve.
Well, I'm not being the maid of honour for your funeral.

JAMIE
I told her you will.

CHICKY walks out the door.

You are right, sis, I have some nerve, but it's shot to hell. Nothing another beer won't fix.

JAMIE takes a long drink.

Lights out.

Scene 11

Thursday, early evening, KRISTA is sitting at the table. A garment bag is draped over the table.

CHICKY comes in from work and half turns to leave when she sees KRISTA.

KRISTA
Hi.

CHICKY
Hi.

KRISTA
I brought your dress. She did a good job hemming it.

CHICKY looks at her puzzled.

Jamie told me you're still gonna be my maid of honour.

CHICKY

He did? Oh what the *(fuck)*. Yeah, yeah.

KRISTA

Thanks for, you know, saying you'll do it.
I think you were right. I should have gone with black heels not white sandals with the fuchsia dress.

CHICKY

It doesn't matter. *(trying again)* It'll look okay. Good.

KRISTA

I'm trying so hard to make everything nice.

> CHICKY *fiddles with a smoke but doesn't light it.*

I was talking to Reg's wife.
She said something I thought I should tell you.

CHICKY

Why would I want to know what she says?
You're thinking like a wife.

KRISTA

Carol said that at the beginning when Reg started seeing you, she never stopped him because you was in love with him, and you was only fifteen and she couldn't bear to see you hurt that bad.

CHICKY

What's that supposed to mean?

KRISTA

She was being nice.

CHICKY

What are you telling me that for?

KRISTA

Don't you want to know it?

CHICKY

I didn't say I'd be your maid of honour, but I'll be your maid of honour, but don't you ever talk to me again!

KRISTA

Chicky… Chicky.

We're doing the groom's family pictures here at 2:30.
You can come get ready at my house if you want.

> *CHICKY ignores her. KRISTA leaves.*

> *Lights down.*

Scene 12

> *Late Thursday night. CHICKY is curled up on the couch, asleep.
> CLARENCE comes in carrying a well-wrapped parcel ready for the
> mail. He takes an apple from the sideboard and a large jack-knife
> from his pocket. He cuts the apple with the knife bringing pieces to
> his mouth on the knife. He watches CHICKY. He goes to the couch
> and kneels beside her. He leans into her, laying his hand reverently
> on her belly.*

> *As soon as his hand touches her, she wakes and pushes him hard
> onto the floor.*

CHICKY
Get the fuck away from me.

CLARENCE
Chicky, I need to talk to you.

> *She sees the knife.*

CHICKY
Jesus, what are you doing with that knife?
What you coming at me with a knife for?

CLARENCE
Here.

> *He gives the knife to her.*

I wasn't trying to hurt you. I was sitting at the table eating an apple
is all, and I got to thinking about you, Chicky.

CHICKY
I *don't* want you thinking about me.
How would you like it if I came at you with a knife? Uh? Uh? I'm the
one who's got reason to do it, too.

CLARENCE
I was eating an apple, Chicky, that's all.

CHICKY
Couldn't hold me down that time, so you gonna do it with a knife.

CLARENCE
I wasn't touching you like that that time.
You thought I was touching you like that?

CHICKY
You crawled into my bed.

CLARENCE
I was missing Trav.
That's all. I swear on Trav's grave that's all.
Did I ever once before, or after that, bother you, Chicky?
No, not once, you know it.

CHICKY
You just had your hand on my zipper.

CLARENCE
No, not on your zipper. I was touching you there, because what you
got inside is precious, Chicky.

CHICKY
What are you raving about?

CLARENCE
Mom's eggs are past it now. She used them goddamn hard anyway.
They won't work for this, not her eggs but you're his half sister and
you're only twenty-five…. Listen! There's this place, Chicky. There's
this place that can clone Travis. Alls you need is good eggs, *your eggs*
would be good for this, and his DNA – I got that.

CHICKY
You're crazy. Nothing's going to bring him back.

CLARENCE
This will.

CHICKY
How can you be so stupid? They're taking your money off you.
That's all they're doing. There isn't a place where they clone people.

CLARENCE
Give me your eggs and I'll show you.

> *CHICKY holds the knife up to her belly.*

CHICKY

What do you want? You want me to slice open my belly and hand them to you like this? Like this?

CLARENCE

They don't need to cut you open, they wash them out.

Then they take the DNA from Trav...

CHICKY

Travis. Travis. I know I'm not a blood relative. I know that, but I've lived in your house since I was three years old. Doesn't that mean anything?

CLARENCE

You was awful good to Travis. You watched him and talked to him. He always wanted Chicky after he got sick.

CHICKY

That's the only thing? What I did for Travis.

Don't you ever see me?

Donalda— *(fuck)* I hate my name.

Has anyone ever seen me my whole life?

CLARENCE

I'd sit and watch him lying next to you, his face whiter than the hospital sheets.

That time, Chicky, that one time I thought if I could lay next to you like he had, maybe I could stand him being...

CHICKY

Dead.

Dead.

Artist's renditions, make-believe cloning places won't change that.

CLARENCE

I'm telling you it will work.

I'm sending his DNA.

CHICKY

Was it you?

Oh, Dad, it wasn't you, was it? Digging up Trav's grave?

CLARENCE

Kevin told you. It was Merv.

CHICKY
> I know what Kev wants to think.
> Where did you get his DNA from, then?

> *CLARENCE picks up the parcel holding it tightly.*

CLARENCE
> We got things around.

CHICKY
> You couldn't dig up his grave, could you, Dad?

CLARENCE
> I got his baby teeth, don't I?

CHICKY
> Is that what you're sending them, you swear it?
> Show me what you're sending them.

CLARENCE
> I don't got to show you nothing.
> Are you going to give your eggs to Trav or not?

CHICKY
> No, Clarence.

CLARENCE
> I thought you loved him.
> I thought, "Chicky will help me bring him home."

CHICKY
> No. *No!*

CLARENCE
> No, but you'll let that one stink them up.
> Yes, I mean Reg.

CHICKY
> Reg isn't you, Clarence, he don't want anything from me. He don't
> ask me to clean his house or clean up his shit. Reg is the one person
> in my life who loves me. Reg. When Travis died he held me, the only
> one, *he held me.* He's loved me since I was fourteen.

CLARENCE
> You ain't fourteen stupid anymore.
> Reg gets the only thing he wants from you every time he spreads
> your legs.

CHICKY
Jesus jumping Christ.

She lunges at him. CLARENCE leaves quickly.

I'll do it, too. I swear I will.

CHICKY puts the knife down on the table.

Lights down.

Scene 13

Saturday afternoon. CHICKY sits at the table sipping wine.
CLARENCE is watching TV. LISSA bursts in with KEVIN close
behind.

LISSA
Hi, Chicky. Where's the bride?

CHICKY
She's fixing her dress, Lissa, what are you doing?

LISSA
Keving said I can watch.

KEVIN
She was already waiting at the church. I told her it was gonna be
a hour before it started. Krista won't care, will she?

CHICKY
Probably.

KEVIN
You sit here, Lissa. Stay out of Krista's way.

LISSA
Okay.

JAMIE and KRISTA come out of the bedroom together.

KRISTA
Well, is your mother coming or not?

CHICKY
She said she would see you at the church, Jamie, or the firehall for
sure. She said to tell you she'll make one hell of a grandmother.

JAMIE

I told you she wouldn't come here for the pictures.

LISSA

I like your bride's dress, Krista.

KRISTA

What is she doing here?

CHICKY

She can watch, can't she, Jamie?

JAMIE

Okay with me.

KRISTA

Nobody is supposed to see the bride before the wedding.

CHICKY

We're all seeing her, one more won't matter.

LISSA

That's a pretty bride veil…

KRISTA

Don't talk to me, Lissa.

Okay. You heard, *(referring to the photographer)* the groom's family first.

> *CLARENCE, JAMIE and CHICKY move as though they are being directed by a photographer. JAMIE sits and the others gather behind him. They hold a pose as KRISTA speaks her monologue. On the last photo CLARENCE holds the picture of Trav to his chest.*

When I was a kid I had a thing about jackets and coats.
Jeez I hated walking the road in a new one. Thinking all those moms looking out their kitchen windows, and people driving by asking themselves, "Now who is that walking down the road."
Like for a day or something nobody would know who I was.
That won't ever happen when Jamie and I are married.
Marrying Jamie, people will always know who I am.

LISSA

Keving, how come you're not in the picture?

KRISTA

> Lissa, shhhhh.
> You'll have to leave.

LISSA

> Pretty shoes.

KRISTA

> Bride and groom with groom's parents… parent.

> *JAMIE, KRISTA and CLARENCE pose.*

> *CHICKY moves away. She starts to speak as they go through the poses.*

CHICKY

> The summer I turned fifteen I did something that people who knew me then would never have believed. It happened at the river. He'd brought a bunch of us swimming 'cause we were haying all day, and hot. Us girls were swimming in our shorts and white T-shirts so our bras would show through. The boys swam through our legs grabbing our crotches saying it was an accident, they was "stuck" or "drowning, honest to fucking God." He sat on the beach smoking, watching me like he had all summer. It was the first time I felt that feeling in my nipples.

> *CHICKY motions LISSA into the photo, which KRISTA resents.*

> He said he needed to see Clarence so he'd drop me off last. Then he asked and I said, "Yes, okay," and he took me back to the river. He brought me down to the water and he said he didn't have any right, he was a married man with kids even. He said I was so beautiful, and he wasn't trying to start anything up with me because that kind of man disgusted him, but he needed me to know that he loved me. And just saying it helped him so much and if he could once in a while tell me that, he'd be okay – never happy now, but okay. Then he stood up and he was walking up the bank. I knew how to stop him. I took off my T-shirt, my bra still damp from the river and I said, "Reg!"
> I did that, shy little me did that, *I* pulled *him* to me.

KRISTA

> Bride and groom, best man and matron… I meant *maid* of honour.

LISSA
Yeah! Keving! Say cheese. *Cheese.*

KRISTA
Kevin.

KEVIN
Shhh, shh.

LISSA
He's my boyfriend. Keving is.

JAMIE
Way to go, Kev.

CHICKY
Don't be sick.

KEVIN
I saw her at the church is all.

KRISTA
We'll never get to the church if we don't get these pictures done.

JAMIE, KRISTA, CHICKY and KEVIN begin to pose.

LISSA
Krista and Jamie can have sex now. Mom says.
Mom says married means having sex. Hens and roosters don't get married. Not dogs. Mr. Bull don't marry the cow – that's silly.
Sex is loud. I can hear the bull when I have to stay put in the house 'cause he's doing his business. I can't go out to the barn, he might think I'm a little cow with a red bum come to visit. No, don't say that, that's a dirty girl. Mom stays put in the house too. She talks *(loudly) like this. "Lissa get the Electrolux and do the front room."* She talks like that 'cause sex is loud. *Sex is loud.*

KRISTA
What did she say?

CHICKY
Lissa, what are you thinking about?

LISSA
Nothing.

JAMIE
Sounds like she's thinking about *something*, eh, Kev?

KRISTA
Jamie!
Bride and groom – *only, Lissa.*

KEVIN
Jame, you should bring the eagle in, put it on your shoulder.

JAMIE
Can't. I let him go.

CHICKY
He can't fly.

JAMIE
I took the bunch of them up to the clear cut this afternoon and let them all go. The cages are empty.

KRISTA
They die anyway.

JAMIE
We're all dying, baby.

KRISTA
Oh that's a nice thing to say on our wedding day.
Like a jinx or something.

JAMIE
When it's my time, put me out in the woods.
If there's any left around here.

KRISTA
Jamie we're going to be late.

They begin to pose.

CLARENCE
I caught a wild fox once
Kept it at the fox farm for years.
It never tamed one bit.
The fox-farm foxes
They was like pets.
Take them to a show
Let them out of their cage
They'd follow behind you
To the show room just like a dog
Jump up on the show table and lay down quiet?

You couldn't expect any animal to be that quiet.
My ones loved to be brushed out
Silver foxes I had.
But that wild vixen one
She never changed.
Until the day she died
Every time I went in the shed to feed her
She'd take a lunge at me.

> *JAMIE and KRISTA are done.*

KRISTA
Maid of honour?

CHICKY
Aren't we done yet?

KRISTA
I paid for the package with the maid of honour and the bride photo.

> *They pose awkwardly in silence.*

JAMIE
Clarence has this story he tells about his tame fox-farm foxes and
this wild vixen he live-trapped and how she used to fight him. He
says, "And every time I fed her she'd lunge at me." He's proud of that
story like it's explaining something. Like it's supposed to mean
something. Anyway, that wild vixen was lunging to get to the door,
to get to that crack of light opened up behind him.
Jesus, some poet should write a poem about those foxes and
Clarence's perforated bowel.

> *The pictures are over.*

KRISTA
Okay, now we're done.
Oh my God, we've got to get to the church.

JAMIE
Any beer at that church, Kevin?

KEVIN
Grape juice.

JAMIE
Better have one for the road.

KEVIN

Better have.

KRISTA

You two are supposed to be at the church now!

CHICKY

I'm going with the guys.

KRISTA

No. The maid of honour rides to the church with the bride. *(teary now)* That's part of the maid of honour's job. It ruins everything if she doesn't.

CHICKY

All right. *(Jesus.)*

LISSA

Here comes the bride, big fat and wide.
Here comes the groom, sweeping up the room.

KRISTA

Kevin, take Lissa with you!
Okay, Chicky help me check my makeup and then we can go.

They go to the bedroom.

JAMIE goes to the coffee table—a small well-polished oval—and rubs his hand over it.

JAMIE

That's one frigging nice table, Kev. That's the same wood?

KEVIN

The log we pulled out from below the swimming hole. Told you, didn't I?

JAMIE

Something that waterlogged had this inside of it.

KEVIN

It's the river what makes it beautiful, Jamie-boy. Brings out the grain of it.

JAMIE

Fucking A, Fucking A plus.

KEVIN

> I got a plan for tonight.

> *JAMIE raises his beer.*

JAMIE

> To the plan.

KEVIN

> I'll catch Mr. Merv on his own tonight.

JAMIE

> You don't have to do it for us, does he, Clarence?

CLARENCE

> Do what?

JAMIE

> Get Merv for digging up Travis's grave. If *he* did it, eh Clarence?

CLARENCE

> I never told nobody to go after nobody.

KEVIN

> I never said you did.
> I'm taking care of it, I told you, Jamie.
> I got a plan.

JAMIE

> Okay, Kev, you handle it.
> Then it will be done.

KEVIN

> Lissa, come on.

> *KEVIN and LISSA leave. JAMIE starts after but stops.*

JAMIE

> Got any fatherly advice for me, Father?

CLARENCE

> I told you what I think.

JAMIE

> Maybe you can tell me what a great son I've been, and how you loved being a father to me. No? Oh, wrong son. I know it was you who dug up his grave.

CLARENCE

What liar told you that?

JAMIE

I saw you at the river hiding something, remember?

CLARENCE

What I did, never hurt nobody.

CHICKY comes out of the bedroom.

JAMIE

I'm sure Travis would love to know you was digging up his bones, sending them off to some swindlers in Scotland to end up in some garbage dump.

CLARENCE

They do not. They *do not.* You forget, I bred foxes all my life, I know what science can be done. They'll get Trav's DNA and put in healthy eggs and he'll be born again.

KRISTA comes out.

JAMIE

No he won't. The funny thing is, if Travis was alive he'd be cursing you out and maybe marrying someone you like even less than Krista. Are we going to the church or not, Krista?

JAMIE and KRISTA leave as CLARENCE shouts at them.

CLARENCE

You don't know that, you don't know that. Trav was never ordinary, not one day of his life. I can help bring him back. I can make all of it right this time. Get him to the doctor before that bastard tumour starts, 'cause it will be inside his brain waiting, but this time I'll know, this time I'll be ready. Chicky, this time I'll be able to save him, right?

CHICKY

I'm *never* doing anything for you *ever again.*

CHICKY leaves.

Lights down.

Scene 14

Late Saturday evening. CHICKY arrives by the river in her bridesmaid dress. She looks around, then sits on the ground. She wipes slow tears from her face. There is the distant sound of police sirens racing through the village. There is some movement in the bushes.

KEVIN
Chicky?

CHICKY
Kevin? I didn't see your car.

KEVIN
I put it down the field a ways.

CHICKY
What are you doing, taking a leak or hiding?

The sound of second police car, the sirens much closer, tearing up the road.

KEVIN
She   did   it!

CHICKY
Kev, get out here.

He comes out.

KEVIN
She called the cops on me.

CHICKY
What's going on?

KEVIN
Merv's wife called the cops.

CHICKY
Why would she do that?

KEVIN
It was his fault, right? Merv. He knew I was after him. He's been lugging his kids with him everywheres 'cause he'd heard I was after him.

CHICKY

Didn't Jamie tell you it was Clarence who dug up Trav's grave?
Clarence and his sick cloning idea.

KEVIN

That don't matter anyway.
I was hurting that bastard for what he done to me.

CHICKY

Oh, Kev, what did you do?

KEVIN

I saw him leave the firehall, and that bitch wife of his wasn't with
him so I knew I had my chance to get him. I chased him up the road
to Reggie's. Merv was flying too. He went off. Hit that big dead elm
in the sod field.

CHICKY

Is he all right?

KEVIN

Yeah. He had a kid with him, Chicky, the boy.
Merv must have made him stay in the car while he was at the dance.
I saw him, Chicky, before I rammed the car I saw him looking at me
out the back window.

CHICKY

Was the boy hurt?

KEVIN

No, he's okay.

CHICKY

You're sure?

KEVIN

Yes – yes. But everywhere I look I see him dead. He's dead when my
eyes are open, he's bleeding and dead when my eyes are closed.

CHICKY

No wonder she called the cops.
You'll be charged…

KEVIN

I know. Merv's got people in there, too, a cousin and some friends in
the county. They'll kill me.

CHICKY
Kev.

ROBBY arrives abruptly. He looks sullen.

Hey, Robby. Pretty late for you isn't it?

ROBBY
No. Bye, Chicky, bye.

CHICKY
Are you okay?

ROBBY
Goodbye, Chicky, bye! You leave, okay.

KEVIN
She ain't leaving so why are you saying goo—

All hell breaks lose. ROBBY comes flying down to the beach, bearing down on KEVIN.

ROBBY emits loud, angry grunts.

ROBBY knocks KEVIN over, sits on him and puts his hands around KEVIN's neck.

CHICKY
Robby.
Let go of Kevin!
Christ, Robby, you're hurting him.

ROBBY continues to hold KEVIN down.

You're killing him! Let him go.

ROBBY
Nooooo! *Nooooo!*

CHICKY
Let go of him, now.
Now!

CHICKY takes the hunting knife out of her dainty evening clutch bag.

If you don't let go of him right now, Robby. *Robby.*
I'm going to cut my hand.
Let go.

I'll cut my hand to the bone.
Look.

> *ROBBY takes his hands away. KEVIN is coughing, holding onto his neck.*

Get off him, Robby.
What's wrong with you?

ROBBY
Make him sorry.

CHICKY
Sorry for what?
Kevin?

KEVIN
Nothing. I didn't do nothing to him. He's frigging crazy.

ROBBY
"Keving kissed me."

KEVIN
Oh, shit.

> *ROBBY moves in to attack again.*

CHICKY
What – Kev what?

KEVIN
One time, on the hand, I kissed her.

CHICKY
Lissa!?

KEVIN
It was a game. She was playing, making the hurts go away.

CHICKY
You hurt her.

KEVIN
No. Chicky. No. She was kissing me better, my bruises.

ROBBY
"Keving my boyfriend."
"Keving my boyfriend."
Lissa said. "Sex is loud."

KEVIN
No way. Chicky, I swear.

CHICKY
She's fourteen.
She is fourteen.

KEVIN
No. Robby? *No!* I kissed her one time on the hand, that's it!

ROBBY hands CHICKY the porcupine.

ROBBY
He give her this present for a kiss.

CHICKY
Jesus.

KEVIN
No. I mean, yes, I gave it to her. *But she kissed me* and I told her you don't kiss a guy if he gives you something.

CHICKY
Did Lissa say he he… had sex with her, Robby?

KEVIN
Oh *come on. No!*

ROBBY
Lissa said, "Keving kissed me."

KEVIN
Nothing, nothing happened.

ROBBY
(clearly angry) He kissed Lissa.

CHICKY
He shouldn't have done that, Robby. God, Kevin.

KEVIN
I'm sorry. Okay, Jesus, I'm sorry.

CHICKY
You did the right thing, Robby. Any guy comes near Lissa, you make him sorry. But don't kill him, because Lissa and Mom need you at home. Right?

ROBBY

Right.

CHICKY

But you can beat him up. You've got my permission to beat the shit out of him.

Okay, Robby?

ROBBY

Okay, Chicky.

CHICKY

You go home, tell Dolores that Kevin kissed her, but that's all.

You tell Mom that he will never ever ever do that again.

You tell him, Kevin.

KEVIN.

Chicky, I'm not gonna…

CHICKY

Tell Robby.

KEVIN

I won't ever kiss Lissa.

CHICKY

You okay?

ROBBY

You okay?

CHICKY

I'm okay. You go home, Mom will be worried about you out so late.

ROBBY

Bye, Chicky.

ROBBY walks with dignity past KEVIN.

CHICKY

Don't talk to me.

KEVIN

They fucked me up, Chicky.

At the camp.

They fucked me up.

CHICKY

We're all fucked up, Kevin. Every last one of us. What happened to you *happened*. None of it gives you the right to mess with Lissa.

KEVIN

I knew kissing *her* was messed up.

CHICKY

'Cause she's slow, Kev? Kissing *any* girl that young is messed up, it screws her up for life. Look at me, I'm twenty-five years old and I got not one person in my life who gives a shit about me 'cause of what *I* did with Reg— *(no, that fuck!)* – *(slowly)* I got no one who cares about me now because of the way Reg looked at me when I was fourteen.

KEVIN

I care about you. I do. I do, a lot.

CHICKY

Listen, Kevin. Mom named me Donald-a for a reason. I figured that much out. *Which* Donald *is it*? I asked her. She wouldn't ever say, only one time—something she hinted—maybe hinted.
Your father was on my list of possible Donalds.

KEVIN

No way.

CHICKY

Before he died, if I was at the store or somewhere he was and your mother wasn't, he'd speak to me every time.

KEVIN

You're not my sister.

CHICKY

(lightly) Krista and I fight like sisters.

KEVIN

No. With you I know I… with you, Chicky, I could… *(do it)*.

CHICKY

Give yourself a chance. Don't let the pricks around here take you down.

> *She kisses his cheek lightly. CHICKY hands him the carving.*
> *KEVIN hands it back to her.*

KEVIN

I carved it for you. Prickly on the outside, soft on the inside, *(pause)* like you, Donalda. *(speaking with a bravado he doesn't really feel)* I hope Dad *was* a cheating bastard.

CHICKY

You are a good guy, Kev.

Sound of a cop car in the distance.

KEVIN

Shit. *(pleading with sound)* I'm sorry, okay. I'm sorry.

CHICKY

Go, go tell them you're sorry.

KEVIN

Before they find me? *(pause)* Will they go easier on me?

CHICKY

If you tell them what Merv did.

KEVIN

No way. I'll go find them, tell them I am sorry what I done tonight, but I'm never telling the cops what happened at the camp.

CHICKY

You going to stay out of his way now?

KEVIN

Merv won't be able to find me, I'll be at the Curl Hole getting that pine out.

CHICKY

Good.

KEVIN

Okay. *Okay.* Take you back to the dance, or are you waiting for... *(Reg)* ?

CHICKY

No. *(pause)* I'm waiting for the right *(pause)* time.

KEVIN

To go back? You and Krista will get over it, you two always do.

CHICKY

Good luck, Kevin.

CHICKY moves in and hugs him. He clings to her, then slowly breaks away and goes up the bank. CHICKY takes off her shoes. A car arrives. As she moves to the river to dip her toes in one last time, JAMIE comes down the bank.

JAMIE
How's it hanging, sis?

CHICKY
What are you doing here?

JAMIE
Down here in the dark is where I fit.

CHICKY
Did you see Kev on the road? He's got himself into a pile of trouble.

JAMIE
A man's got to do what a man's got to do.

CHICKY
That is so stupid.

> *JAMIE opens the beer he is carrying. He indicates that he is right in this matter.*

Where's Krista?

JAMIE
Waiting in the car. She don't want to ruin that white thing she's wearing.

CHICKY
Nice, you guys are fighting. Wow, nine hours of wedded bliss.

JAMIE
(shrugs) Hey what can I say?
What are you doing down here?

CHICKY
I'm waiting 'til I'm sure Clarence will be asleep then I'm getting my clothes and getting out of there. I won't live in that house, not after what he did.

JAMIE
Where are you going to?

CHICKY
I have no idea – far, far away.

JAMIE
Taking Reg with ya?

CHICKY
I'm a lay to him.
I'm what makes him a big man at the firehall.
I use to think it was love when we'd sneak out of the dance for
a quick screw in the back seat of his car. I'd walk into that hall after
and think they was all seeing that I had won something.
Tonight I wanted to hurt him like I've been hurting for… *(ten
years).*
When he came out to the car I was gonna stick your hunting knife
into him, not kill him, but stick it somewhere that I could be the
only explanation. "Chicky did it. Did you hear? Chicky did it."

JAMIE
Why didn't ya?

CHICKY
He never came out. Promised he would but he didn't.

JAMIE
Hey. Say the word and I'll lay the beating on him he deserves.

CHICKY
He isn't worth it. Reg is the worst kind of a shit. *(at the moon) You
fucking shit!* That's what I'm saying tonight, but I'm scared if I'm
here tomorrow and he comes around smiling, I'll fall back down the
Reg well.
So I'm going.

JAMIE
Good, sis. Good on you.

CHICKY
What about you?

JAMIE
What about me?

CHICKY
What if I go out to where the heli-logging training is? Get set up in

a place. You and Krista can come stay with me while you're doing your training.

JAMIE
(mildly) Sounds good, sis.

CHICKY
I mean it.

JAMIE
(mildly) F'ing A.

CHICKY
You're married now, we can leave together.

JAMIE
Yup… next spring.

CHICKY
Why not now?

JAMIE
Do you know how much it costs to fly a helicopter from this life to a new life?

CHICKY
But you said you're going to get the money together, right?

JAMIE
Twenty-five thousand, no *forty thousand* dollars 'cause we're flying at night.

CHICKY
Fuzzy…

JAMIE
Yeah…

CHICKY
Doesn't mean you can't do it. Krista can get a job. She's not totally helpless.

JAMIE
Ah ah ah. Answer me this. If helicopter A left helipad B at C midnight and helicopter X left helipad T at 8 a.m. flying F *backwards*, how much math would you have to know to get to the goddamn fucking moon.

He throws the beer bottle towards the moon.

CHICKY
Jamie…

JAMIE
Hey, I know the answer and the answer is "Fucked if I know."

CHICKY
You can learn the math. You're not dumb.

JAMIE
Yeah, yeah, yeah.

CHICKY
I can't wait until spring, Jamie. I'm leaving tonight while I am too scared to stay.

She picks up her handbag.

You coming back to the car? Your bride is waiting.

JAMIE
In a minute. Nature calls. You were a mother of a sister to me, Chicky.

CHICKY
You're Krista's problem now.

CHICKY moves in to give him a hug but he neatly avoids it.

JAMIE
You going so I can take a whiz, or what?

CHICKY
See ya. I'll call.

CHICKY goes up the bank.

Lights down.

Scene 15

Lights up. KRISTA makes her way down the bank in her wedding dress. She has JAMIE's white tux jacket draped around her shoulders. The bottom of the dress is muddy.

KRISTA

Jamie, I've been waiting forever. Look at my dress. Mud won't come out either.

Jamie we got to get back to the dance. Jamie! You said you was only stopping to have one smoke then we was going back.

KRISTA sees his wedding shoes next to the shore.

Jamie. Jamie.

Lights up on "the high," the top of the bridge frame. JAMIE, drunk, sways slightly as he looks down at her.

JAMIE

Nice dress. You look like a ghost.

KRISTA

It's wrecked, thanks to you.

Get down here and get your shoes on.

JAMIE

You ain't the boss of me. *(laughs)*

KRISTA

We got our wedding guests at the firehall.

JAMIE

They ain't the boss of me, either.

KRISTA

You didn't have to get mad at me.

You were the one telling everyone we're going to B.C.

I never said I would go to B.C., Jamie.

JAMIE howls like a coyote.

Don't be doing that, you're not jumping.

Jamie, you hear me, you are not jumping off the high on our wedding night. Jesus, Jamie, it's dark! You can't see where you're jumping to.

JAMIE howls again, louder, wilder.

If you jump, Jamie, I will never talk to you again.

You listen. I won't, not one word I won't. I'll be like Chicky's being to me, for the rest of our lives.

I won't talk to you, Jamie, you frigging, Jamie.

JAMIE howls but it is broken off. JAMIE disappears from sight.

JAMIE
Jesus Jesus Jesus sweet fucking Christ
The waters never seemed so far away.
I ain't drunk enough! Jesus, I ain't drunk enough.
Ain't I in the water yet?
Where's that fucking hole?

I see it now.
I see it.
Fucking Christ I'm missing it.
It's way the fuck over there.
It's too fucking late. I'm hitting the water.

It's like entering Krista when she's dry and I'm hard.
Pop pop pop my backbones are whipping back my neck
Snapping my head like a chain strung too tight letting go.
Jesus, is this it?
This is it then?
Krista out there standing by the water got her hands cupped like
she's gonna say my name.
Gonna call me back.
I stare up, up through the surface waiting for Krista to say,
waiting for her words to break through the blue of it.

But then the water is like a screen and I'm watching our life together
played out.
I'm seeing it, Krista, our life   you and me.
I see that baby you got curled inside of you that you don't know
about yet, only he's four years old.
He's four and he's just shit himself because of the beating I laid on
you
So I slap you again to teach him not to shit himself.
And I see that Christmas, I'll put the tree and all the presents out in
the snow
Because you forgot to get my beer
And it's Christmas Eve and I don't got my goddamn beer.
Krista
Krista call my name
And I'll come out of the water
And we'll go back to the dance.

Next week when we know about the baby in you, Earl's gonna call me up. Tells me he's gonna sell the tree processor. Tells me if I buy it he'll hold the mortgage for me. And I do it 'cause maybe it's the way a dumb ass can get somewheres. And I'm inside the machine every night, I'm doing it, taking the woods down in two counties 'cause there is always the payment, the goddamn *fucking (this is JAMIE's most deeply felt moment – it is of a fox forced to chew off its own leg to escape the steel trap)* payments.

The alcohol's always right there, too, so I don't have to think about why I never went away that time.

The bird in the cage is me.

I am the bird of death, with the soul of the woods in my beak.

Only I can't say that stuff except with my fists.

One night I must have been changing a hose they tell ya.

I must've disconnected the kill switch on the seat they say.

I took a stupid chance and she shifted and I lost my balance or

I jumped and over she went on to me they tell you, and the cops are at the door telling you I'm dead.

But you ain't sad, you're scared.

When they give you my wallet you find the ticket to the jewellery store in town.

You find out I got forty dollars down on a heart ring for you for Christmas. When you put that ring on your finger the bad things, the ugly things is all gone.

You pay it off and you wear it telling the boys how it was a surprise and how much I really loved you.

And I can't say if I hadn't died that day if I ever would have paid it off 'cause maybe you would have made me mad.

Or I needed to fix the truck and I might have gone in and got my money back.

I see it all, Krista.

I see it all.

If you call my name, just once

If you say it, say "Jamie"

My backbone strings itself together

Heals itself just like that *(snaps fingers)* and I'll come out of the river,

You'll dance in your wedding dress

And everything will happen just as I've said.

Alls you got to say is "Jamie"
Say "Jamie" and all this will come to pass.

There is a very long pause as KRISTA waits for JAMIE to break the surface.

KRISTA
I swear to God.
I swear to God.

I told you not to.
I told you.
You ain't coming up
You ain't coming up.
You   shit
I hate you.
You fucking fucker.
Please.
Please.
Please.

Jamie.

JAMIE walks out to her. He picks up his shoes. He holds out his hand. KRISTA notices the knife on the beach. She picks it up and hands it to JAMIE. As they walk over the bridge JAMIE is staring straight ahead and KRISTA is staring up at his face.

The end.